KT-369-569

THE
RUDIMENTS OF MUSIC

by

WILLIAM LOVELOCK
D.MUS. (LOND.)

London
G. BELL & SONS, LTD

First published 1957

Reprinted 1962, 1964, 1966, 1969, 1970, 1971, 1972, 1974

ISBN 0 7135 0744 6

Printed in Great Britain by
Billing and Sons Limited, Guildford and London

CONTENTS

FOREWORD

There is nothing new to be said on the subject of this book. All that the writer can do is to arrange the chapters in what he feels to be the most suitable and logical order, and to make his explanations as simple and lucid as possible. This I have tried to do.

In some cases, *e.g.* Time and Intervals, a subject has been dealt with in two short chapters rather than in one long one. The lengthy and comprehensive chapter is apt to give the student indigestion; a small dose of information followed by appropriate exercises is grasped and retained with less trouble and greater certainty.

The appendices contain information which is in no way necessary to the elementary student, but which may usefully supplement his knowledge when he has reached the stage of being ready to assimilate it. The teacher is obviously the best judge of this.

I have tried throughout to keep in mind the examination candidate; hence the inclusion of reference to certain specific types of examination question.

My sincere thanks are due to my colleagues Miss Enid Langley, F.T.C.L., L.R.A.M., A.R.C.M., and Wilfrid Dunwell, B.A., B.Mus., Ph.D., for their kindness in reading and commenting on the original draft.

W. L.

CHAPTER 1

PRELIMINARY

1. Musical sounds differ in the following ways:

    (i) Duration
    (ii) Pitch
    (iii) Accent
    (iv) Intensity
    (v) Timbre

2. **Duration** means simply the length of a sound, this length being measured in beats. In all music there is a regular, even beat or pulsation, and the length of a sound means how many beats, or what fraction of a beat, it lasts.

3. **Pitch** is the height or depth of a sound.

4. **Accent** means stress or emphasis; some sounds are more strongly accented than others.

5. **Intensity** means the degree of loudness or softness.

6. **Timbre** means the quality of a sound. The timbre of the sound produced by a pianoforte differs from that of a violin, and both differ from that of, say, a trumpet or an oboe.

7. Musical notation is the method by which sounds and their differences are expressed on paper—the various signs and symbols which are used for this purpose.

CHAPTER 2

DURATION OF SOUNDS

1. A sound is represented in notation by a sign called a **note**, and sounds of different lengths are shown by notes of different shapes.

2. The longest note in normal use is the **semibreve**, written thus: ○

    Shorter notes, in descending order of value, are:

    Minim—𝅗𝅥
    Crotchet—♩
    Quaver—♪
    Semiquaver—𝅘𝅥𝅯
    Demisemiquaver—𝅘𝅥𝅰
    Hemidemisemiquaver—𝅘𝅥𝅱

3. The **minim** is a round, open note like a semibreve with an upright stroke attached. This is called its 'stem', the round part of the note is the 'head'.

    The **crotchet** is like a minim with its head filled in, making it a black note.

    The **quaver** is like a crotchet with a 'tail' (or 'hook') attached to its stem.

    The **semiquaver** has two tails, the **demisemiquaver** three and the **hemidemisemiquaver** four.

4. Stems may be upwards or downwards, according to rules to be explained later. Upward stems are always to the right of the head, downward ones to the left:

    Tails are always to the right of the stem—♪ or ⌐—and may be either straight, as shown above, or curved, thus:

    The latter are most common in printed music; in manuscript the straight tails are generally neater and quicker to write. Stems should be thin strokes, tails rather thicker.

5. When several notes with tails—quavers, semiquavers, etc. —occur in succession, it is usual to join their tails so as to form groups of notes, thus:

Ex. 1. ♩♩ ♫♫♫ 𝅘𝅥𝅯𝅘𝅥𝅯𝅘𝅥𝅯𝅘𝅥𝅯

The rules governing such grouping are explained in Chapter 5.

6. Each of the notes listed in para. 2 is worth twice the value of the note below it, that is, it represents a sound lasting twice as long. A semibreve is worth two minims, a minim is worth two crotchets, a crotchet is worth two quavers, and so on. A semibreve is therefore worth four crotchets, eight quavers, etc. A minim is worth four quavers, eight semiquavers, etc.

7. The following table shows how many of one note are equal to another note:

2 𝅘𝅥𝅰 = 𝅘𝅥𝅯   2 𝅘𝅥𝅯 = ♪   2 ♪ = ♩   2 ♩ = ♩   2 ♩ = ♩   2 ♩ = ♩   2 ♩ = o

4 𝅘𝅥𝅰 = 𝅘𝅥𝅯   4 𝅘𝅥𝅯 = ♪   4 ♪ = ♩   4 ♩ = ♩   4 ♩ = o

8 𝅘𝅥𝅰 = ♪   8 𝅘𝅥𝅯 = ♩   8 ♪ = ♩   8 ♩ = o

16 𝅘𝅥𝅰 = ♩   16 𝅘𝅥𝅯 = ♩   16 ♪ = o

32 𝅘𝅥𝅰 = ♩   32 𝅘𝅥𝅯 = o

64 𝅘𝅥𝅰 = o

8. Another method of naming notes, used largely in America, is as follows:

The o is called a **whole-note**, and hence:

♩ is a half-note

♩ is a quarter-note

♪ is an eighth-note

𝅘𝅥𝅯 is a sixteenth-note

𝅘𝅥𝅰 is a thirty-second-note

𝅘𝅥𝅱 is a sixty-fourth-note

9. Yet another method is that in which the crotchet is called

a **'one-beat note'**, since it is often used to represent one beat.   From this the following results:

○ is a four-beat note

𝅝 is a two-beat note

♪ is a half-beat note

♪ is a quarter-beat note

♪ is an eighth-beat note

♪ is a sixteenth-beat note

The weakness of this system is that the crotchet is by no means always used to represent a one-beat sound.

10. Longer than the semibreve, twice its length, is the **breve**, written as either ‖○‖ or ▭ .
This is only rarely used nowadays, but is not infrequently met with in older music.

11. A note may be lengthened by the use of the **tie** or **bind**. This is a curved line which goes from the head of one note to the head of the next, thus:

(a) 𝅝 𝅘𝅥   (b) 𝅗𝅥 𝅘𝅥

At (a) the sound would be held for the combined value of the minim and the crotchet.   At (b) it would be held for the combined value of the crotchet and the semiquaver. Note that a tie must join the *heads* of the notes, not their

tails.   𝅝 𝅘𝅥 is incorrect.

12. Another way of lengthening a note is by placing a **dot** after it.   This adds half to the original value.   Thus, 𝅝 is worth two crotchets; 𝅝. (called a 'dotted minim') is worth three crotchets.

13. A second dot adds on half the value of the first dot, so that the two dots together add on three-quarters of the original value.   Thus:

𝅝 is worth four quavers—

𝅝. is worth six quavers—  , the dot add-

ing the value of two quavers.

♩.. called a 'double dotted minim', is worth seven

quavers— ♪ ♪ ♪ ♪ ♪ ♪ ♪ ♪ , the second dot adding

on one more quaver.

Each dot adds on half of what is immediately in front of it.

QUESTIONS AND EXERCISES ON CHAPTER 2

1. How are the different lengths of sounds shown in musical notation?
2. Give the names of the various notes, beginning with the longest and ending with the shortest.
3. Write each of the following notes twelve times. Vary the direction of the stems, and ensure that they are all neatly and correctly formed:
    Crotchet
    Semiquaver
    Semibreve
    Demisemiquaver
    Minim
    Hemidemisemiquaver
    Breve
    Quaver
4. How many quavers are there in a semibreve?
    How many semiquavers are there in a crotchet?
    How many minims are there in a breve?
    How many demisemiquavers are there in a crotchet?
    How many crotchets are there in a semibreve?
    How many hemidemisemiquavers are there in a quaver?
5. Write the following groups of notes, joining their tails:
    Four quavers
    Eight demisemiquavers
    Two hemidemisemiquavers
    Six semiquavers
6. Give the usual American names for the following:
    Crotchet, demisemiquaver, semibreve, quaver, minim, semiquaver, hemidemisemiquaver
7. Give the English and the American names for each of the following:

8. Describe the Tie and give an example of its use.

9. Explain the effect of placing a dot after a note.
10. Explain the effect of placing two dots after a note.
11. By using dots, write:
    (a) a note worth three crotchets
    (b) a note worth six demisemiquavers
    (c) a note worth seven semiquavers
    (d) a note worth twelve quavers
    (e) a note worth fourteen semiquavers

CHAPTER 3

PITCH OF SOUNDS

1. The pitch of sounds is described by a series of letter-names, known as the **musical alphabet.** These are seven in number—A, B, C, D, E, F, G—each being one step higher in pitch than the one before it. Music employs, however, a much wider range than a mere seven sounds, so the alphabet is repeated throughout this range. After reaching G we begin again on A, and this process is repeated as many times as may be necessary. The distance or **interval** between any note and the next one of the same letter-name, either upwards or downwards, is called an **octave.**

2. An Interval is defined as the difference in pitch between two sounds. The smallest interval used in European music is called a **semitone** (=half-tone). In the musical alphabet the intervals from E to F and from B to C are semitones. The intervals between the other next-door notes, C to D, D to E, etc., are whole tones.

3. The pitch of a note is shown by its position on the **stave** or **staff.** This consists of five parallel lines drawn across the page:

Ex. 2.

Notes are written either on (*i.e.* across) the lines, or in the spaces between them. The higher the position of the note on the stave, the higher its pitch.

Ex. 3.

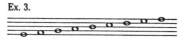

Ex. 3 shows a rising series of next-door notes from the bottom to the top of the stave.

4. When a passage moves as in ex. 3, always to the next-door note, it is called **conjunct movement**, that is movement by steps, or stepwise movement. If the notes are not

next-door to each other (as in ex. 6) it is **disjunct movement** or movement by leap.

5. The stave itself is not sufficient to show the exact name and pitch of a note. In ex. 3 we can see that the second note is higher than the first, the third higher than the second, and so on; but we have no means of knowing their letter-names or their exact pitch. To show this a sign called a **clef** is used. A clef is a sign placed at the beginning of every stave, which fixes the pitch of one line, and so fixes that of all the other lines and spaces.

6. The two clefs most in use are the G and the F, for which the signs are respectively 𝄞 and 𝄢 or 𝄢. Either of the two forms of the latter may be used. The ·G clef, 𝄞, is also called the **treble clef**, and the F clef, 𝄢 𝄢, the **bass.**

7. The G clef curls round the second line of the stave and fixes this line as the G above Middle C. **Middle C** is in the middle of the piano keyboard and lies at about the middle of the series of sounds usually employed in music.

Ex. 4.

This is called a treble stave.

8. If we now rewrite ex. 3 with a G clef, we can see that the names of the notes are as shown in ex. 5, beginning from the E above middle C.

Ex. 5.   E   F   G   A   B   C   D   E   F

This is called a treble stave.

9. The notes of the treble stave are best learned by separating the lines and the spaces, thus:

Ex. 6.   Lines   Spaces

E   G   B   D   F   F   A   C   E

10. The F clef has its two dots one on each side of the fourth line of the stave, and fixes it as the F below middle C.

Ex. 7.

This is called a bass stave.

N.B. Do not omit the two dots of this clef and always ensure that they are correctly placed.

11. Ex. 3 with an F clef reads thus:

Ex. 8. G A B C D E F G A

Separating the lines and the spaces we have:

Ex. 9.

Lines   Spaces

G B D F A   A C E G

12. If the two staves are now placed one above the other we have the following:

Ex. 10.

E F G A B C D E F

G A B C D E F G A

This leaves a gap between the A at the top of the bass stave and the E at the bottom of the treble. A D may be placed hanging below the lowest line of the treble, and a B resting on the top line of the bass, thus:

Ex. 11.

D E F

G A B

But middle C is still missing. It is inserted by the use of a **leger line.** This is a short horizontal line which acts as an extension of the stave and a note may be written across,

B

above, or below it. We can now complete the whole series of notes from the lowest line of the bass to the top line of the treble:

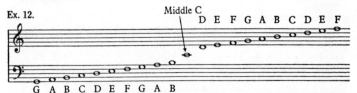

Ex. 12.

Middle C

D E F G A B C D E F

G A B C D E F G A B

13. From the above example we can see that middle C is the connecting link between the two staves. If the treble and bass staves are moved closer together and the middle C line included, we obtain an outsize stave of eleven lines, which is called the **great stave:**

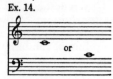

Ex. 13.

This would make clefs unnecessary; its middle (sixth) line is known as middle C and all the other lines and spaces can be calculated from it. But it is obviously impossible to read from such a stave, which is merely a theoretical possibility (see Appendix).

14. With the two five-line staves, middle C is not written midway between as in ex. 12, but either immediately below the treble or immediately above the bass, thus:

Ex. 14.

or

15. The range of notes given in ex. 12 is not sufficient to cover all our needs. Higher or lower notes are made available by the use of leger lines above or below the staves, thus:

Ex. 15.

F G A B C D E F G A B C

The second note, G, resting on top of the stave, counts as a 'space' note, and from there the notes are alternately across or above the leger lines. Ex. 15 takes us to an octave below the highest note on the piano keyboard, and to use still more leger lines would obviously make reading still more difficult. For the very high notes an **'octave sign'** is used. This is *8va* · · · · · · · ¬,[1] and when placed over a passage of notes it indicates that they are to be played one octave higher than written. Thus:

is played as

and

represent the top four notes of the full-scale piano keyboard.[2]

16. The bass stave is extended by leger lines below it:

The sign *8ve* . . . . ⌟ or *8va bassa* placed below a passage means that it is to be played one octave lower. '*Bassa*' is the Italian word for 'below'. Thus:

---

[1] *8va* is an abbreviation of the Italian word *Ottava*.
[2] Some pianos extend only as far as A.

is played as:

and the lowest notes of the piano, down to the bottom **A**, would be written thus:

17. A figure *8* below a note in the bass clef means that it is to be played *with* its octave below.

means:

Sometimes '*con 8*' or '*con 8ve*' are used.   ('*Con*' means 'with'.)

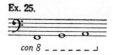

means:

18. The treble stave may be extended downwards, and the bass upwards, by leger lines. We have already seen that the middle C line does this.

Ex. 27.

In these cases the leger lines as it were borrow from the other stave.

19. The term middle C identifies the C which lies between the treble and bass staves. Other C's are conveniently known as follows:

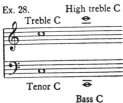

Ex. 28. High treble C
Treble C
Tenor C
Bass C

20. The correct direction of the stems of notes must be watched. The basic rule is that if the note is above the middle line of the stave, its stem should be downwards; if below the middle line, the stem is upwards. On the middle line it may be either up or down. Ex. 29 (a) is correct; (b) is incorrect.

Ex. 29.
(a)   (b)

When a number of quavers, semiquavers, etc., have their tails joined, the direction of the stems depends on the distance of the highest and lowest notes of the group from the middle line. In

Ex. 30.

the lowest note, G, is only two notes below the middle line, but the highest, F, is four notes above it. The highest note is farther above the middle line than the lowest is below it. The highest note, as it were, wins, and the stems of the whole group are downwards. Similarly, in:

the low G is farther below the middle line than the high G is above it, so stems are upwards. Note that it is the *distance* from the middle line that matters, not the number of notes in the group which are above or below it.

QUESTIONS AND EXERCISES ON CHAPTER 3

1. Explain the musical alphabet.
2. What is an octave?
3. Which letters in the musical alphabet represent sounds which are only a semitone apart?
4. What does a stave consist of? What is its purpose?
5. Define (*a*) Conjunct Movement, (*b*) Disjunct Movement.
6. What is a clef, and what is its purpose?
7. Draw twelve G and twelve F clefs on a stave, taking care that they are correctly placed and correctly shaped.
8. Write these notes on a treble stave:
   G on a line
   C in a space
   F on a line
   D on a line
   Middle C
   E in a space
   D below the stave
   A in a space
   B on a line
   G above the stave
9. Under each of these notes write its letter-name:

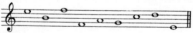

10. Write these notes on a bass stave:
    D on a line
    B above the stave

B on a line
A in a space
F on a line
F below the stave
C in a space
A on a line
G on a line
G in a space

11. Under each of these notes write its letter-name:

12. What is a leger line?
13. Under each of these notes write its letter-name:

14. Write these notes at their actual pitch, taking care to use the proper number of leger lines in each case. Under each note write its letter-name:

15. Write these notes at their actual pitch, taking care to use the proper number of leger lines in each case. Over each note write its letter-name:

16. Write out the following as they would be played:

17. On a treble stave write the G below middle C;
On a bass stave write the E above middle C.
18. Rewrite the following with the stems in the proper directions:

CHAPTER 4

RESTS

1. A period of silence in music is shown by a sign called a **rest.** There is a rest corresponding in value to each kind of note, as follows:

Name	Note	Rest
Breve		
Semibreve		
Minim		
Crotchet		
Quaver		
Semiquaver		
Demisemiquaver		
Hemidemisemiquaver		

The relative values are the same as those of the corresponding notes.

2. Care is needed in the formation and placing of rests on the stave. The breve rest is an upright block filling the space between the third and fourth lines of the stave.

The semibreve rest is a horizontal block hanging below the fourth line.

The minim rest is a horizontal block resting on the third line.

To distinguish between the semibreve and the minim rests remember that the **S**emibreve rest is **S**uspended from the line, while the **M**inim is **M**ounted on it. S—S, M—M.

Avoid the common fault of writing either of these two as

Ex. 32.

3. Either of the two given forms of the crotchet rest may be used. ꞃ is the older form, and is more convenient for use in manuscript; ꝴ is more common as the printed form. To avoid confusing the crotchet rest ꞃ with the quaver ꝰ, remember that the ꞃ is open to the right, as is the letter C, the first letter of crotchet. The head of the ꝰ is to the left of the stem, and so is the head of small q, the first letter of quaver. The heads of ꞃ and ꝰ are placed in the third space, as is shown in para. 1.

The shorter rests, semiquaver, etc., follow the quaver in having their heads to the left of the stem.

The quaver note has one tail; its rest has one head.

The semiquaver note has two tails; its rest has two heads. And so on.

4. Rests, like notes, may be dotted, the dot adding on half the value. A silence worth three quavers could thus be written as:

Ex. 33.

Equally, it could be written as:

Ex. 34.

that is, crotchet plus quaver. Rests are never tied.

QUESTIONS AND EXERCISES ON CHAPTER 4

1. How is silence indicated in musical notation?
2. Write, on a stave, a complete set of rests, beginning with the longest and ending with the shortest.
3. Name these rests:

4. On a stave write the following:
   (*a*) a rest worth four quavers
   (*b*) a rest worth eight crotchets
   (*c*) a rest worth two demisemiquavers
5. Show two ways of indicating a silence worth
   (*a*) three crotchets
   (*b*) three semiquavers

CHAPTER 5

SIMPLE TIME; GROUPING OF NOTES AND RESTS

1. In all music there is a regular, even beat or pulse, and these beats are in groups of two, three or four. The first of each group is accented, that is, it is stronger than those which follow it. Time in music deals with the grouping of the beats and their value.

2. If the beats are grouped in twos they are alternately strong and weak:

S W S W S W
1 2 1 2 1 2

This may be compared with the tramp of soldiers on the march—*left*, right, *left*, right, *left*, right.

Grouping in twos produces what is called **duple time.**

3. If the beats are grouped in threes we have a strong one followed by two weak ones:

S W W S W W S W W
1 2 3 1 2 3 1 2 3

To think of the swing of a waltz may help to make this clear. Grouping in threes gives **triple time.**

4. When beats are grouped in fours the first has a strong accent, the third a medium one; the second and fourth are weak:

S W M W S W M W S W M W
1 2 3 4 1 2 3 4 1 2 3 4

This is **quadruple time.**

5. In musical notation the 𝅗𝅥, the ♩, or the ♪ may be used to represent a one-beat sound, at the choice of the composer. The ♩ is the most common.

6. To show the position of each strong beat an upright line, called a **barline,** is drawn across the stave immediately in front of it. Duple time with crotchet beats appears thus:

Ex. 35.

(S   W   S   W   S   W)

The music between two consecutive barlines is called a **bar** or **measure,** and ex. 35 therefore contains three whole bars. Ex. 36 shows the barring in triple and quadruple times with crotchet beats:

Ex. 36.
Triple

(S   W   W   S   W   W   S   W   W)

Quadruple

(S W M W S W M W S W M W)

7. At the end of a piece, or at the end of an important section of it, a **double barline** is used.

Ex. 37.

It does not necessarily come before an accented beat and may occur anywhere in a bar.

8. To show how many beats there are in a bar, and what their value is, a sign called a **time-signature** is used, being placed at the beginning of the first line of the music, immediately after the key-signature.[1] A time-signature consists of two figures, one above the other. The upper figure shows the number of beats in each bar. The lower figure shows the value of each beat as a part of a semibreve.

Lower figure 2 indicates minim beats, since there are two minims in a semibreve.

Lower figure 4 indicates crotchet beats, since there are four crotchets in a semibreve.

Lower figure 8 indicates quaver beats, since there are eight quavers in a semibreve.

The signature $\frac{2}{4}$ therefore means two crotchet beats in a bar; $\frac{3}{8}$ means three quaver beats; $\frac{4}{2}$ means four minim beats.

Note that a time-signature is *not* a fraction; there is no stroke between the two figures.

[1] See chap. 8.

9. So far, therefore, we have the following time-signatures available:

Of these, $\frac{2}{8}$ is so rarely used as to be negligible. $\frac{4}{8}$ is also rare. $\frac{2}{4}$, in which the bar contains the same total amount, four quavers, is used instead.

10. The sign **C** is sometimes used to mean $\frac{4}{4}$. **¢**, rather less common, may mean either $\frac{2}{2}$ or $\frac{4}{2}$.

11. In all these times the beat divides into two of the next smaller note. Crotchet beats divide into two quavers, minim beats into two crotchets and quaver beats into two semiquavers. When the beat is divisible into two equal parts the time is called **Simple.** The full description of $\frac{3}{4}$ time would therefore be: 'Simple triple time with crotchet beats'; that of $\frac{4}{2}$ would be: 'Simple quadruple time with minim beats'.

12. Notes and rests are grouped (that is, arranged) so as to show clearly the number, value and position of the beats in each bar, in accordance with the time-signature. When beats are subdivided into smaller notes with tails, these tails must be joined so as to show the beats, thus:

Ex. 38.

When a beat is subdivided into very short notes, as at the end of the $\frac{4}{4}$ bar above, it is clearer to use one long tail to show the whole beat and shorter ones to show the half beats. It is far easier to read this than one solid mass of eight demisemiquavers:

Ex. 39.

13. In $\frac{2}{4}$ and $\frac{3}{4}$ times a whole bar of quavers may be grouped on one tail, but in $\frac{4}{4}$ the position of the medium accent on the third beat must be shown by a new group:

Ex. 40.

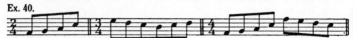

Similarly with semiquavers in $\frac{3}{8}$. They may also be shown as at (*c*) in ex 41.

Ex. 41.

14. Single notes worth two, three or four beats are allowable:

Ex. 42.

Also notes worth one and a half or one and three-quarter beats:

Ex. 43.

15. With two exceptions, no rest of greater value than one beat may be used. These exceptions are:

(*a*) A two-beat rest may be used for the first two or the last two beats of a bar of quadruple time, *but not for the second and third beats of the bar*.

(*b*) A whole bar of silence is shown by a semibreve rest, whatever the time-signature, except in $\frac{4}{2}$, when a breve rest is used. (This is logical enough, since a whole bar of $\frac{4}{2}$ adds up to the value of a breve.)

Ex. 44.

(*a*), (*b*) and (*c*) are correct; (*d*) is wrong—the position of the third beat accent is not shown. (*e*) is also wrong, as a two-beat rest is never used in any kind of triple time. The correct version is at (*f*).

16. The accent may be moved from a strong beat on to what is normally a weak one by **syncopation.** This word means 'displaced accent', a weaker beat receiving the accent which normally belongs to a strong one. Syncopation is usually effected by placing a long note on what is normally a weak beat and holding it over the following accented beat:

Ex. 45.

The sign $>$ indicates accent and is used to mark notes which are to be strongly stressed.

17. In completing a bar with rests (a common kind of examination question), the rule to remember is:

Complete each beat before starting the next, and each part of a beat before starting the next part.

To do this correctly we must (*a*) decide on how many beats there are in the bar, and what is the value of each beat, this being shown by the time-signature, and (*b*) decide how each beat divides up. Suppose we have to complete the following by adding rests between the given notes:

Ex. 46.

The signature $\frac{3}{8}$ tells us that there are three quaver beats in the bar. Each of these quavers divides into two semiquavers, four demisemiquavers, and so on.

The semiquaver at the beginning must be the first half of the first beat, so we add a semiquaver rest to complete this beat. The demisemiquaver at the end of the bar must be the last quarter of the third beat, so we first complete the last half of this beat by adding a demisemiquaver rest in front of the note, and then a semiquaver rest in front of this to complete the whole beat. In the middle of the bar we must then place a quaver rest for the second beat, and the result is:

Ex. 47.

18. Another example:

Complete the following bar by adding rests, in proper order, after the last note.

Ex. 48.

Four minim beats are shown by the signature, each dividing into two halves (crotchets), four quarters (quavers), eight eighths (semiquavers). The first beat is already occupied by the initial crotchet and two quavers. The two semiquavers which follow are equal to a quaver, the first quarter of the second beat. They must be followed by a quaver rest to complete the first half of this beat, and then by a crotchet rest to complete the whole. This leaves the third and fourth beats, which are the *last two beats of a bar of quadruple time* and are therefore to be covered by a two-beat rest, *i.e.* a semibreve (see para. 15). The solution is therefore:

Ex. 49.

19. When a piece begins on some other beat than the first of a bar it is said to begin with an incomplete bar. In such a case it is usual to arrange that the final bar of the piece is also incomplete, and that its contents added to those of the incomplete first bar shall add up to the value of a whole bar according to the time-signature. Thus:

Ex. 50.

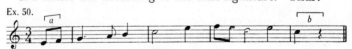

(*a*) and (*b*) together add up to a complete bar of $\frac{3}{4}$.

QUESTIONS AND EXERCISES ON CHAPTER 5

1. Explain (*a*) duple time, (*b*) triple time and (*c*) quadruple time.
2. In what way does the accentuation of a bar of quadruple time differ from that of two bars of duple time?
3. What is a barline?
4. What is a double barline?
5. What is the use of a time-signature? Explain how it is constructed.
6. Explain the meanings of the following time-signatures:

   $\frac{3}{4}$, $\frac{4}{8}$, C, $\frac{4}{2}$, $\frac{3}{8}$, $\frac{4}{4}$, ¢

7. Give the time-signatures which mean the following:
   (*a*) Simple triple time with quaver beats
   (*b*) Simple quadruple time with minim beats
   (*c*) Simple duple time with crotchet beats
8. Give the correct time-signature for each of these complete bars of music:

9. Rewrite each of the following complete bars of music, grouping the notes correctly in accordance with the time-signatures:

10. What rest is used for a whole bar of silence?
11. When is it correct to use a two-beat rest?
12. Rewrite the following correctly, and state why the given examples are incorrect:

13. What is meant by syncopation? Give an example.
14. What rule is to be followed when completing a bar with rests?

C

15. Complete these bars by adding rests, in correct order, after the
last note in each case:

16. Complete these bars by adding rests, in correct order, *before* the
first note in each case:

17. Complete these bars by adding rests, in correct order, *between*
the given notes in each case:

18. Give the correct time-signature for each of these complete bars
of music. In each case describe the time as explained in para. 11.

CHAPTER 6

COMPOUND TIME AND GROUPING

1. It is sometimes necessary that beats shall be divisible into three smaller notes instead of two. This can be effected by the use of an **irregular note-group** called a **triplet.**

2. An irregular note-group occurs when a note is divided into some other number of smaller notes than are normal. For example, a crotchet normally divides into two quavers, but it can be 'irregularly' divided into three by the use of the triplet. The definition of a triplet is 'three notes to be played in the time of two of the same kind'. The three notes are grouped together and a figure 3 is placed above or below them to indicate the irregular group, thus:

Ex. 51.

The curved line ⌒ or ⌣ is called a **slur** and its use over or under the figure is customary. Do not confuse it with the tie. The square bracket ⌐¬ as at (*b*) is sometimes used and is much to be preferred, since it avoids the risk of confusion with the slur, which has various uses.

3. The use of the triplet serves well enough if only the occasional beat is to be divided into three. But if we need a whole piece with this subdivision the irregular group is not used. If we use dotted notes for beats, the division into three smaller notes will be regular. Thus:

Ex. 52.

is replaced by:

Ex. 53.

and:

Ex. 54.

by:

Ex. 55.

and so on.

4. When the beats are dotted notes, the time is called **compound.** Ex. 52 is simple duple time with crotchet beats; ex. 53 is compound duple time with dotted crotchet beats. Ex. 54 is simple triple time with quaver beats; ex. 55 is compound triple time with dotted quaver beats. The dotted notes are the beats and the three smaller notes into which each beat divides are called **pulses.**

5. The use of dotted beats involves a new set of time-signatures. In simple time, as we already know, the upper figure shows the number of beats in each bar and the lower figure the value of each beat as a part of a semibreve. Ex. 52 is therefore in $\frac{2}{4}$ time. In ex. 53 we still have two beats in the bar, each being a dotted crotchet. But a dotted crotchet cannot be expressed as a part of a semibreve. There are three quavers in a dotted crotchet and eight in a semibreve, so that a semibreve is worth $2\frac{2}{3}$ dotted crotchets. To use a time-signature like $\frac{2}{2\frac{2}{3}}$ is obviously cumbersome, to say the least.

In any form of compound time each beat divides into three pulses, and *the time-signature shows the number and value of these pulses.* In ex. 53 there are six pulses, each being a quaver—an eighth of a semibreve. The time-signature is therefore $\frac{6}{8}$. Similarly, in ex. 55 we have nine semiquaver pulses, and the signature is $\frac{9}{16}$.

6. Every kind of simple time has its corresponding form of compound time, obtained by dotting its beats. Ex. 53 with two dotted crotchet beats is the compound form of ex. 52 with two undotted crotchet beats.

7. To find the number of *beats* in a bar of compound time, divide the upper figure of the signature by 3. To find the value of each beat, divide the lower figure by 2 and dot the result. For example, $^{12}_{8}$. 12 divided by 3 is 4; four beats in the bar. 8 divided by 2 is 4, which indicates crotchet beats. So we have four dotted crotchets in the bar, which could be fully described as 'compound quadruple time with dotted crotchet beats'.

8. The complete list of compound time-signatures is:

9. The principles of grouping of notes and rests are the same as in simple time. Note that when the first two pulses of any beat are silence, a single two-pulse rest is used; but if the second and third pulses are silence, then two separate one-pulse rests are needed.

(*a*) and (*b*) are correct; (*c*) is wrong.

A whole-beat rest may be written either as two pulses plus one pulse, as on the second beat of (*b*), or as a dotted three-pulse rest, as on the second beat of (*d*). The rule already given regarding two beat rests also applies.

Ex. 57.

(*a*) shows a two-beat rest for the third and fourth beats of a quadruple bar;

(*b*) shows two separate one-beat rests for the second and third beats;

(*c*) is wrong.   Compare ex. 44 (*d*).

10. Completing bars with rests is done in the same way as in simple time.   For example:

Ex. 58.

$\frac{9}{8}$ means three groups of three quavers.   The given demi-semiquaver is the first quarter of the first quaver.   Add a demisemiquaver rest to complete the first half, and then a semiquaver rest to complete the whole pulse.   This leaves the second and third pulses of the beat as silence, so two separate quaver rests are needed—see para. 9.   The remainder of the bar consists of two whole beats of silence, which, the time being triple, must be written as two separate one-beat rests.   Hence:

Ex. 59.

11. Besides the triplet there are other irregular note-groups. The most common are:

(*a*) **Duplet**—two notes in the time of three of the same kind.

(*b*) **Quadruplet**—four notes in the time of three or six of the same kind.

(*c*) **Quintuplet** or **quintolet**—five notes in the time of three or four of the same kind.

(*d*) **Sextuplet** or **sextolet**—six notes in the time of four of the same kind.

(*e*) **Septolet**—seven notes in the time of four or six of the same kind.

The duplet and quadruplet occur in compound time only.

The sextolet in simple time only. Quintolet and septolet may occur in either simple or compound time.

The quadruplet may be written in either of two ways.

(*a*) in the note-values of the three notes it replaces (ex. 60 (*b*));

(*b*) as the four notes which would together make up the undotted beat in the corresponding form of simple time (ex. 60 (*c*)).

Ex. 60.

Note that in every case the appropriate figure is placed over or under the irregular group.

Note also the use of the words 'of the same kind' in all the definitions. Merely to say that 'a triplet is three notes in the time of two' might lead to such a ridiculous suggestion as 'three crotchets in the time of two semiquavers'.

12. Rather rarely pieces with five or seven beats in a bar may be encountered. The former is called **quintuple** time, the latter **septuple.** They may be either simple or compound. In quintuple time the beats are grouped as either two plus three, or three plus two:

1 From Debussy's String Quartet. Reproduced by kind permission of Durand et Cie., Paris.

In septuple time the grouping of beats is three plus four or four plus three.

QUESTIONS AND EXERCISES ON CHAPTER 6

1. Define (*a*) irregular note-group, and (*b*) triplet.
2. Write (*a*) a triplet of crotchets and (*b*) a triplet of semiquavers.
3. How is the continual use of the triplet avoided when it is necessary to have beats divisible by three?
4. Distinguish between simple time and compound time.
5. Distinguish between beat and pulse in compound time.
6. Explain the difference between a simple time-signature and a compound time-signature.
7. Give the time-signatures of the compound forms of:

$$\frac{3}{4}, \quad \frac{2}{2}, \quad \frac{4}{8}, \quad \frac{3}{2}, \quad \frac{4}{4}$$

8. Give the time-signatures of the simple forms of:

$$\frac{6}{8}, \quad \frac{9}{16}, \quad \frac{12}{4}, \quad \frac{9}{8}, \quad \frac{6}{16}$$

9. At the beginning of each of these complete bars of music write its proper time-signature:

10. When may a two-pulse rest be used in compound time? When is it incorrect to use one?
11. At the beginning of each of these complete bars of music write its proper time-signature:

12. Complete each of these bars by adding rests in proper order after the last note in each instance:

13. Complete each of these bars by adding rests in proper order *before* the *first* note in each instance:

14. Complete each of these bars by adding rests in proper order *between* the given notes in each instance:

15. Group twelve semiquavers correctly as (*a*) a bar of $\frac{3}{4}$ time, (*b*) a bar of $\frac{6}{8}$ time, and (*c*) a bar of $\frac{12}{16}$ time.

16. Write the following, (*a*) in $\frac{6}{8}$ time, (*b*) in $\frac{3}{4}$ time. Do not alter the order, nor the relative lengths of the sounds.

17. Rewrite the following with correct grouping according to the given time-signatures:

18. Define the following:
   Quadruplet, septolet, duplet, quintolet, sextolet, giving an example of each.

19. Define quintuple and septuple times.

CHAPTER 7

SHARPS, FLATS, ETC.

1. The notes already described in Chap. 3 can each be raised or lowered a semitone. (Semitones may be found on the piano keyboard by moving from any note to the very next one to it, whether black or white, upwards or downwards.) The sign for raising a note a semitone is called a **sharp**—♯; that for lowering a note a semitone is a **flat**—♭. Sharps and flats are placed in front of the notes they affect, and on the same line or space:

Ex. 62.

2. In writing sharps and flats always see that they are clear and of reasonable size. The lines forming the sharp should be clearly separated, and the body of the flat should be well rounded. The following are quite common faults and are to be avoided:

Be especially careful that sharps and flats are exactly opposite the notes to which they refer, and avoid such carelessness as:

Ex. 63.

instead of:

Ex. 64.

In ex. 63 the sharp and flat are actually meaningless.

3. To restore a sharpened or a flattened note to the pitch of its ordinary letter-name a sign called a **natural**—♮—is used.

Ex. 65.
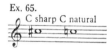
C sharp C natural

(The white notes of the piano are familiar examples of these 'naturals'.)

4. A note may be raised two semitones (i.e. a whole tone) by the use of the **double-sharp**—×, or lowered two semitones by the **double-flat**—♭♭. These signs, again, must be in front of the notes to which they refer, and on the same line or space.

Ex. 66.
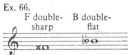
F double-sharp   B double-flat

Note that the sign for double-sharp is *not* ♯♯—a common error. If a note is already sharp, then a double-sharp raises it another semitone. If already flat, the double-flat lowers it another semitone.

5. To change a note from double-sharp to sharp, only the sharp sign is needed. Formerly it was customary to use a 'double cancellation' by inserting both a natural and a sharp. This is unnecessary.

Ex. 67

G double-sharp   G sharp   not

Similarly in turning a double-flat note into a flat one:

Ex. 68

B double-flat   B flat   not

A ♮, of course, restores a × or ♭♭ note to its 'natural' (white-note) pitch.

Ex. 69
F double-sharp   F natural   D double-flat   D natural

6. ♯, ♭, ×, ♭♭, ♮ written in front of notes are called **accidentals.**
Where the note concerned has a leger line, that line does
not touch or pass through the accidental.

Ex. 70

is correct;

Ex. 71

is not.

7. Remember that an accidental affects only the one line or
space on which it is placed. For example, in:

Ex. 72

the lower F is sharp, but the upper one is not, though for
safety's sake it would be usual to place a ♮ in front of it.

8. The effect of an accidental lasts until the end of the bar
in which it occurs, unless it is contradicted. Thus, in the
first bar of ex. 73 all the F's are sharp, but the F in the
second bar is natural, even though not so marked. If the
natural note occurs at the beginning of the next bar, as
at (*b*), it is usual to insert the contradiction to be on the
safe side.

Ex. 73

9. The same sound may have more than one name. For
example, we already know that from E to F is a semitone,
and so also is the interval from E to E sharp. So E sharp
and F are two different names for the same sound. Similarly, C double-sharp is two semitones above C natural,
that is, a whole tone. From C to D is also a whole tone,
so C double-sharp and D are the same sound. When two
notes with different letter-names represent the same sound

they are called **enharmonic** or **enharmonic equivalents.** The complete list of enharmonic equivalents can best be made clear by reference to the piano keyboard.

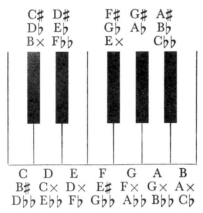

From this it will be seen that all but one of the twelve sounds within the octave can have three different letter-names. But although all these names are theoretically possible, most of the double-sharps and double-flats are never used in musical notation.

QUESTIONS AND EXERCISES ON CHAPTER 7

1. Give the signs and their names which (*a*) raise a note a semitone, (*b*) lower a note a semitone.
2. Under each of these notes write its name:

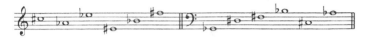

3. Write these notes as quavers on the treble stave:
    G flat, B sharp, F sharp, D flat, E sharp, C flat, Middle C sharp, A flat.
4. Write these notes as minims on the bass stave:
    A sharp, Middle C flat, F flat, D sharp, G sharp, B flat, E flat.
5. Write the sign called a natural, and explain its use.

6. Explain and give the signs for double-sharp and double-flat.
7. Under each of these notes write its name:

8. Write these notes as semibreves on the treble stave:
   F double-sharp, B double-flat, Middle C double-flat, G double-sharp.

9. Write these notes as semiquavers on the bass stave:
   E double-flat, Middle C double-sharp, D double-sharp, A double-flat.

10. What is an accidental? How long does its effect last?

11. Give other names for the following sounds:
   F, G double-sharp, B flat, A sharp, E double-flat, C sharp, D double-sharp, F flat.

12. Define enharmonic equivalents.

CHAPTER 8

MAJOR SCALES

1. In its simplest form a scale is a series of notes in alphabetical order from any note to its octave, upwards or downwards. The word scale is derived from the Latin *scala*, a ladder, and a scale is a kind of 'ladder' of notes.
2. Scales are of two kinds, **diatonic** and **chromatic.** In a diatonic scale some of the steps or 'degrees' are a tone apart, some are a semitone; in a chromatic scale all the next-door degrees are a semitone apart.
3. There are two kinds of diatonic scale—**major** and **minor,** the difference between them depending on the order in which the tones and semitones occur.
4. The note from which a scale begins—the foundation note, as it were—is called the **keynote** or **tonic.** In a major scale the semitones occur between the third and fourth, and the seventh and eighth notes above the tonic. (Note that scale degrees are always reckoned *upwards* from the tonic.) The scale of C major, that is, the major scale with C as its tonic, is thus:

Ex. 74

T=whole tone. S=semitone.
The interval between the first and third degrees of the scale is two whole tones, known as a major 3rd (see Chap. 11). Hence the name 'major scale'.
5. Every diatonic scale consists of two groups of four next-door notes, as shown by the brackets above ex. 74. These groups are called **tetrachords.** In a major scale the two tetrachords have the same order of tones and semitones, i.e. tone, tone, semitone, and are thus 'similar tetrachords'. A tetrachord may be defined as 'the lower or upper half of a diatonic scale, four notes in alphabetical order'. The tetrachords in the major scale are separated by a whole

tone between the top note of the lower one and the bottom
note of the upper one, that is, between the fourth and fifth
degrees of the complete scale. This is called the **'tone of
disjunction'**—which simply means the tone which separates
them.

6. Every major-scale tetrachord can belong to two scales,
being the upper half of one and the lower half of another.
But if we take the upper tetrachord of the scale of C major
and add another one above it, using no sharps or flats,
we obtain:

Ex. 75

In this there is a semitone between the sixth and seventh
degrees from the lowest note of the scale, instead of between
the seventh and eighth, so it is not a true major scale. To
correct this a sharp must be placed before the F, putting
the upper semitone in its proper place:

Ex. 76

This produces a major scale beginning on G and is known
as the scale of G major.

7. Repeating the same process and beginning a scale with the
upper tetrachord of G major we shall need a sharp before
the seventh note of our new scale to keep the correct order
of tones and semitones:

Ex. 77 Scale of D Major.

This process can be continued, each time beginning a new
scale with the upper tetrachord of the previous one and
adding a new sharp before the seventh note from the bottom,
until we have used up all the seven possible sharps, reaching the scale of C sharp major:

Ex. 78

8. When a piece of music is written using as its basis the notes of a certain scale, it is said to be in the **key** of that scale. So that a piece which is based on the notes of the scale of, say, D major, is 'in the key of D major'.

9. The tonic of each new scale with sharps is the fifth note of the preceding one. The order of keys with sharps, starting from C major, is:

C   G   D   A   E   B   F♯   C♯

1   2   3   4   5   6   7

Each new scale needs one more sharp than that preceding it, and that sharp is applied to its seventh degree—the note below the upper tonic. The order in which these sharps occur is:

F   C   G   D   A   E   B

The complete list of major scales with sharps is:

Ex. 79

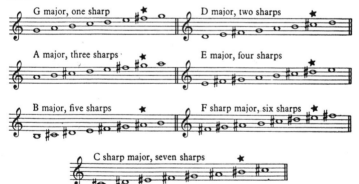

Each scale includes all the sharps in the scale preceding it, and the new sharp is in each case marked by a ★.

10. Reversing the procedure shown above, we can take the lower tetrachord of the scale of C major and use it as the *upper* one of a new scale, thus:

Ex. 80

But this gives a lower tetrachord consisting of three consecutive whole tones, and the 'tone of disjunction' has become only a semitone. This is corrected by placing a flat before the B, the top note of the lower tetrachord, producing the scale of F major:

Ex. 81

For each new scale with flats, a new ♭ must be placed before the fourth note from the bottom—the top note of the lower tetrachord. Using the lower tetrachord of the scale of F Major as the upper one of a new scale we obtain the scale of B flat major, which requires an E flat:

Ex. 82

11. Continuing the same process until we have used up all the seven possible flats, we reach the scale of C flat major:

Ex. 83

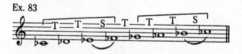

12. The tonic of each new scale with flats is the fourth note of the preceding one, and the order of keys is:

C   F   B♭   E♭   A♭   D♭   G♭   C♭
  1   2   3   4   5   6   7

Each new scale needs one more flat than that preceding it, and that flat is applied to its fourth degree. The order in which these flats occur is:

B   E   A   D   G   C   F

This is the exact reverse of the order of sharps.
The complete list of major scales with flats is:

Ex. 84

Each new scale includes all the flats in the scale preceding it, and the new flat is in each case marked by a *.

13. If the scale concerned contains sharps, the piece is said to be 'in a sharp key'; if it contains flats, then the piece is 'in a flat key'.

14. Sharps and flats used as above, that is, placed in front of the notes to which they refer, are, as we already know, called accidentals. But too many accidentals make reading very difficult, and to simplify matters, those sharps or flats which belong to a scale are grouped together in the form of a **key-signature.** This is placed at the beginning of each stave of music, immediately after the clef. It shows that the notes to which it refers are always to be sharp or flat, unless otherwise marked by an accidental.

15. G major needs an F sharp, so its key-signature consists of a ♯ on the F line (ex. 85 (*a*)). F major needs a B flat, and its key-signature consists of a ♭ on the B line (ex. 85 (*b*)).

Ex. 85

16. The following is a complete list of major key-signatures with their tonics:

Ex. 86

Note (i) The sharps or flats in key-signatures are always placed as shown in ex. 86. It is incorrect, for example, to write the signature of A major thus:

Ex. 87
or

(ii) Leger lines are never used in key-signatures.

(iii) A sharp or a flat in a key-signature affects *all* notes of the same letter-name, all over the stave, unlike an accidental which only affects one line or space. The sharp in the signature of G major (see ex. 86), affects not only the F on the line, but all other F's on the stave;

and the same applies with all other key-signature sharps or flats.

17. For convenience in reference the degrees of a diatonic scale are given **'technical names'**. The first degree we already know as the **tonic,** which is the most important note of the scale. Next in importance[1] is the fifth degree, known as the **dominant.**

Thus, in C major:

Ex. 88

The fourth degree above the tonic is also the fifth below the upper tonic. It is the same distance below the tonic as the dominant is above it, and so is called the **subdominant,** an 'under-dominant'. (*Sub* is Latin for under or below.)

Ex. 89

Midway between the first and fifth degrees lies the third, called the **mediant**—the 'midway' note. Correspondingly, midway between the tonic and the subdominant lies the third degree downwards, the **submediant** or 'undermediant'.

Ex. 90

The second degree of the scale, one step above the tonic, is the **supertonic** (*super* means above). The seventh degree, one step below the tonic, has a strong feeling of wanting to lead up to the tonic, and so is called the **leading-note.**[2]

[1] There is a logical reason for this relative importance, but to explain it would be lengthy, and also incomprehensible to the beginner.

[2] In America it is customary to reserve the term 'note' for the written sign. A sound is called a 'tone', so that the seventh degree of a scale is called the 'leading tone'.

Ex. 91

Here is a complete list of the technical names applied to the scale of C major:

These names apply correspondingly in *all* scales, whether major or minor. The third note of any scale is always the mediant, for example. In G major this would be the note B; in E flat major it would be G; and so on.

18. A scale need not necessarily begin on its tonic, though the scale degrees are *always reckoned upwards* from that note. Suppose we have to write the scale of E flat major beginning on the leading-note, with key-signature. The answer must be:

Ex. 93

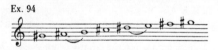

The semitones are marked by slurs.

In writing such a scale without key-signature, be especially careful to place the sharps or flats before the proper notes, according to the signature. For example, B major beginning on the submediant. B major has F♯, C♯, G♯, D♯, A♯, so each of these notes must have a sharp before it.

Ex. 94

19. Finally, remember that sharps and flats in signatures must always be written in the order given in paras. 9 and 12. Examination candidates occasionally give them in the order

in which they occur as the ascending scale is played, so
that the signature of B major may appear thus:

Ex. 95

QUESTIONS AND EXERCISES ON CHAPTER 8

1. What is a scale?
2. Define (*a*) a diatonic scale, (*b*) a chromatic scale.
3. What are the two kinds of diatonic scale? On what does the
   difference between them depend?
4. What is the tonic or keynote of a scale?
5. Which degrees of a major scale are a semitone apart?
6. What is the name given to an interval of two whole tones?
7. What is a tetrachord? What is the order of tones and semitones
   in the two tetrachords of a major scale?
8. What is the tone of disjunction?
9. How is the scale of G major connected with the scale of C major?
10. What do we mean when we say that a piece of music is 'in the
    key of E major'?
11. Give the correct order of 'keys with sharps', and state also the
    order in which these sharps occur.
12. Write these scales, placing sharps in front of the notes which
    need them, and marking the semitones by slurs:
    A major, F sharp major, D major, B major, C sharp major.
13. How is the scale of F major connected with the scale of C major?
14. Give the correct order of 'keys with flats', and state also the
    order in which these flats occur.
15. Write these scales, placing flats in front of the notes which need
    them, and marking the semitones by slurs:
    E flat major, G flat major, B flat major, D flat major, C flat
    major.
16. To each of the following add the necessary sharps or flats to
    make them into major scales beginning with the given first note
    in each case:

17. What is a key-signature?

18. Write the key-signatures of the following major keys, and after each write its tonic as a semibreve. Give them with both treble and bass clefs:

E, A flat, G flat, B, B flat, F sharp, D, E flat.

19. After each of these major key-signatures write its tonic as a crotchet.

20. Write, in minims, one octave ascending of each of the following major scales. Add the correct key-signatures and mark the semitones by slurs:

E flat, D, F sharp, A flat, E, C flat.

21. Write, in separate semiquavers, one octave descending of each of the following major scales. Add the correct key-signatures and mark the semitones by slurs:

D flat, E, G flat, B, F, C sharp.

Use the F clef.

22. Give the technical names of the degrees of the scale.

23. Write, on a treble stave, one octave ascending of each of these major scales. Insert the correct key-signatures and mark the semitones by slurs:

B flat beginning on the mediant

E beginning on the leading-note

G flat beginning on the dominant

A beginning on the submediant

24. On a bass stave write, in quavers, one descending octave of each of these major scales. Use no key-signatures, but place sharps or flats before the notes which need them. Mark the semitones by slurs:

G beginning on the supertonic

C flat beginning on the subdominant

B beginning on the leading-note

25. Write, with key-signatures, one octave, ascending and descending, of each of the following major scales. Group the notes according to the stated time-signatures; insert the necessary bar-lines, and complete the final bar with rests in proper order:

A flat major in semiquavers, $\frac{6}{8}$ time

D major in quavers, $\frac{9}{8}$ time

E major in demisemiquavers, $\frac{9}{16}$ time

CHAPTER 9

MINOR SCALES

1. In Chap. 8 it was mentioned that the major scale is so called because its third degree is a major 3rd above the tonic. In the minor scale the third degree is only a tone and a half above the tonic, a *minor 3rd.* Hence the name **'minor scale'.** Formerly it was customary to refer, for example, to 'the key of C with the major 3rd', or 'the key of A with the minor 3rd',[1] rather than, as nowadays, C major and A minor.

2. There are two forms of minor scale, the **harmonic** and the **melodic.** The former is so called because from it are derived the harmonies most frequently used in the minor key. The latter, as will be seen, is primarily for melodic purposes.

3. In the harmonic minor scale semitones occur between the second and third, the fifth and sixth, and the seventh and eighth degrees. The sixth and seventh degrees are separated by an interval of three semitones, known as an **augmented 2nd.** The other degrees lie a whole tone apart.

4. If we take the note A as tonic and write an octave of notes above it, we have:

Ex. 96

This has semitones between its second and third and its fifth and sixth degrees, but not between the seventh and eighth. To correct this, the G—seventh note—must be raised a semitone by means of a sharp:

[1] Or 'with the greater third' and 'with the lesser third' respectively.

This gives us the scale of **A harmonic minor,** and is the pattern for all harmonic minor scales.

5. The **melodic minor scale** is designed to avoid the augmented 2nd which occurs between the sixth and seventh degrees of the harmonic form, which was formerly considered to be unvocal, if not unmusical. The ascending melodic scale differs from the descending one. Ascending, the semitones lie between the second and third, and the seventh and eighth degrees; descending, between the sixth and fifth, and the third and second.

Scale of A melodic minor.

This is the pattern for all melodic minor scales.

6. Minor scales, whether harmonic or melodic, are connected with major scales in two ways:

    (*a*) A minor scale may have the same key-signature as a given major scale, but will begin on a different tonic;

    (*b*) A minor scale may have the same tonic as a given major scale, but will have a different key-signature.

7. When a major and a minor scale have the same key-signature they are known as **relative.** The minor is the **'relative minor'** of the major, and the major is the **'relative major'** of the minor.

8. The relative minor of any given major scale has for its tonic the sixth degree (submediant) of that major scale. Thus, the relative minor of C major is A minor, that of G major is E minor, that of F, major is D minor, and so on. C major has no key-signature, so A minor has none. G major has one sharp, so E minor has one sharp. F major has one flat, so D minor has one flat.

Ex. 99

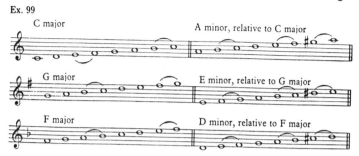

Note that the sharpened leading-note of the harmonic minor has the same letter-name as the dominant of its relative major.

9. The order of sharps and flats in minor key-signatures is the same as that for major keys (see Chap. 8, paras. 9 and 12).

10. When a major and a minor scale have the same tonic they are known as **tonic major** and **tonic minor.** C minor is the 'tonic minor of C major'; E major is the 'tonic major of E minor'.

11. The tonic minor of a given major scale has in its key-signature *three more flats or three fewer sharps* than that major scale. (Note that this is the simplest way to learn and remember minor key-signatures.) Thus, F major has one flat, so F minor has one plus three, that is, four—**B, E, A, D.** B major has five sharps, so B minor has five minus three, that is, two—**F and C.**

12. Two minor keys appear to be exceptions to this, but actually they are not. D major has two sharps, so D minor should have two minus three, which is 'minus one'. 'Minus one sharp' is 'plus one flat', which is the signature of D minor. Similarly, G major has one sharp. One minus three is 'minus two', i.e. 'plus two flats'.

13. As with major keys, the tonic of each successive minor key with sharps is the fifth degree of the one preceding it. The tonic of each successive minor key with flats is the fourth degree of that preceding it. The following table of minor key-signatures with their tonics should make this clear, and shows the order of keys:

Ex. 100

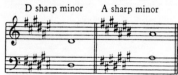

The same key-signature is used for both forms of any given minor scale. For example, C harmonic minor and C melodic minor both have the same three flats in their signatures. But the harmonic form will need a B natural both ascending and descending, while the melodic will need an A natural and a B natural ascending, but not descending.

14. In every harmonic minor scale with a key-signature, the seventh degree above the tonic must be raised a semitone by an accidental, in order to make the semitone between it and the upper tonic. This is done both ascending and descending, and is called 'sharpening' the leading-note. But note that the sharp sign ♯ is not always the right one. To 'sharpen' merely means to raise a semitone, so that if the note concerned is flat according to the signature, then it will be 'sharpened' by using a ♮. If the note is already

sharp according to the signature, then a double-sharp (×)
will be needed.

15. In melodic minor scales with key-signature, the sixth and
seventh degrees are sharpened in the ascending form, but
lowered again to their key-signature pitch in descending.
See ex. 101 below. If the descending form is written without being preceded by the ascending, then no accidentals
are needed.

16. The technical names of the degrees of a scale, tonic, supertonic, etc., apply equally to both forms of the minor scale.

17. The following is a complete list of harmonic and melodic
minor scales with key-signatures. The semitones are
marked by slurs.

Ex. 101

C melodic minor

F melodic minor

B flat melodic minor

E flat melodic minor

A flat melodic minor

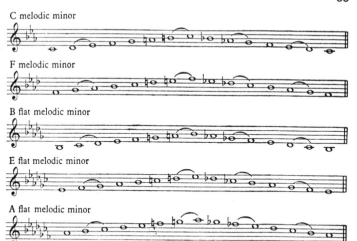

18. In writing a minor scale without key-signature, all the sharps or flats which would be in the key-signature must be inserted as accidentals, allowing for the sharpening of the leading-note. For example, in writing the scale of C harmonic minor the flats for the E and the A will be inserted, but the flat for the B, which appears in the signature, will be omitted, since B is the seventh degree and must be sharpened. To sharpen a flat note we make it natural, but in this case no ♮ sign will be needed since without a key-signature the B is natural anyway. Hence:

Ex. 102

Similarly with, say, G sharp melodic minor. Its key-signature has five sharps, F, C, G, D, A. The sixth degree, E, must be sharpened by a ♯. The seventh degree is already sharp, according to the signature, so to sharpen it we must use a ×. Descending, these two degrees must be restored to what they are according to the signature. Hence:

Ex. 103

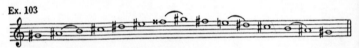

19. In writing a scale which does not begin on its tonic, be careful to put the accidentals needed to sharpen the seventh, or the sixth and seventh degrees in front of the correct notes *counting upwards from the tonic*. For example, F harmonic minor, with key-signature, beginning from the subdominant; (*a*) is correct, but (*b*)—a common kind of error in examinations—is wrong.

Ex. 104

Scale degrees are always reckoned *upwards from the tonic*, and the seventh degree from F is E, not A. Although the scale is written beginning from B flat, F is still the tonic. Similarly with a melodic minor scale, say C sharp without key-signature, starting on the supertonic:

Ex. 105

The sixth and seventh degrees from C sharp are A and B, to which the necessary sharps must be applied in ascending, and cancelled descending.

20. In writing any diatonic scale it is important to remember that each letter name must be used *once and once only*, in alphabetical order. Some students seem to have an abhorrence of such notes as B sharp or F double-sharp, so that the scales of C sharp minor and G sharp minor are apt to be written thus:

Ex. 106

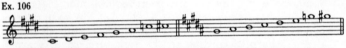

These are incorrect since the alphabetical sequence is broken. As written here, the C sharp scale has no B, but two C's, and the G sharp one has no F but two G's.

QUESTIONS AND EXERCISES ON CHAPTER 9

1. Why is the minor scale so called?
2. Between which degrees of the harmonic minor scale do semitones occur? What is the interval between the sixth and seventh degrees?
3. Between which degrees of the melodic minor scale do semitones occur?
4. How are minor scales connected with major scales?
5. Give the order of keys of (*a*) minor scales with sharps, (*b*) minor scales with flats.
6. Write the following harmonic minor scales, one octave ascending, with key-signatures. Mark the semitones by slurs:
    G, F sharp, B flat, E, B, D sharp, E flat.
7. Write the following melodic minor scales, one octave ascending and descending, with key-signatures. Mark the semitones by slurs:
    D, C sharp, A flat, C, A sharp, G sharp.
8. Write one octave ascending and descending of each of the following scales, without key-signatures. Mark the semitones by slurs:
    B harmonic minor, F melodic minor, B flat melodic minor, C sharp harmonic minor.
9. Write one octave, ascending and descending, of each of the following minor scales. Use the correct key-signatures and mark semitones by slurs:
    F harmonic, beginning on the leading-note
    E melodic, beginning on the mediant
    A sharp harmonic, beginning on the submediant
    B flat melodic, beginning on the supertonic
10. To each of the following add the necessary accidentals to turn them into minor scales beginning on the first note given:

11. Write, with key-signatures, one octave, ascending and descending, of each of the following minor scales. Group the notes according to the stated time-signatures; insert the necessary barlines, and complete the final bar with rests in proper order:
    B, harmonic, in quavers, $\frac{9}{8}$ time
    F melodic, in semiquavers, $\frac{6}{16}$ time
    F sharp harmonic, in demisemiquavers, $\frac{12}{16}$ time

CHAPTER 10

CHROMATIC SCALES

1. A **chromatic scale** is one which proceeds entirely by semitones. It thus uses every possible sound between a note and its octave. Unlike a diatonic scale, some letter-names have to be repeated, since the chromatic scale has thirteen notes to the octave, but there are only seven letter-names.

2. Semitones are of two kinds—**diatonic** and **chromatic.** The diatonic semitone occurs in diatonic scales (as well as in chromatic ones), but the chromatic semitone is found in the chromatic scale only.

3. In a diatonic semitone the two notes have different letter-names, e.g. E to F, F sharp to G, B to A sharp.
   In a chromatic semitone the two notes have the same letter-name, but one or both will need an accidental, e.g. C to C sharp, B flat to B natural, G flat to G double-flat.
   The distinction is easily remembered thus:
   *D*iatonic—*D*ifferent.
   Both words begin with a D.

4. Chromatic scales, like minor ones, are of two kinds, **harmonic** and **melodic.** But whereas there is a difference in some of the actual sounds of the two kinds of minor scale, in the chromatic the difference is in notation. There can be no difference in sound, since every possible sound is used, and all are the same semitone interval apart.

5. The **harmonic chromatic scale** uses the notation from which the 'chromatic harmonies' of a key are derived; the melodic chromatic scale is designed for ease in reading.

6. Every key has its own proper notation for the chromatic scale. The notation of the harmonic form is derived as follows:
   Taking C as tonic, the scale will contain all the notes of C major:

Ex. 107

From both forms of the minor scale are added the notes which differ from those of the major scale, i.e. E flat, A flat and B flat. These, being flattened notes, are written to the left of their naturals:

Ex. 108

The necessity for the natural signs should be obvious. This leaves whole tones between C and D, and F and G. The former is filled in by adding a flattened second degree, D flat, and the latter by a sharpened fourth degree, F sharp. Hence:

Ex. 109

This is called the **'harmonic chromatic scale of C'.** Diatonic semitones are marked 'D', chromatic ones 'C'. Note that the tonic and dominant notes—the two most important notes of the diatonic scale—appear once only; all the other degrees appear twice. The same method of derivation applies, whatever the tonic.

7. The above method of building the scale, while showing its derivation, is too cumbersome for ordinary use. Chromatic scales may be written with either the major or the minor signature of the key, and two simple rules suffice:

(i) *With the major key-signature.* Write the major scale and add a flattened 2nd, 3rd, 6th and 7th degrees and a sharpened 4th.

(ii) *With the minor key-signature.* Write the scale *without accidentals*, and add a flattened 2nd degree and a sharpened 3rd, 4th, 6th and 7th.

Remember that to flatten a note means to lower it a semitone, not necessarily by means of a ♭; and that to sharpen a note means to raise it a semitone, not necessarily by means of a ♯. Flattened notes go to the left of the original ones, sharpened notes to the right.

8. Suppose we have to write the harmonic chromatic scale of A flat with the major signature. The first step is to write the major scale, leaving space for the insertion of the extra notes:

Ex. 110

The 2nd degree is B♭, so a 'flattened 2nd' is B♭♭. A flattened 3rd is C♭, flattened 6th F♭, and flattened 7th G♭. We now have:

Ex. 111

Each of these extra notes (given as crotchet heads for clarity) must have its accidental contradicted.

The 4th degree of our original scale is D♭, so sharpened it becomes D♮. This goes to the right, the upper side, of the D♭, so no contradiction of the ♮ is needed. Hence the complete scale:

Ex. 112

9. A harmonic chromatic scale with the major signature always has nine accidentals ascending.

10. In descending the flattened notes go to the right and the sharpened one to the left. (Always remember that scale degrees are counted from the bottom upwards.) Thus, in the key of A flat:

Ex. 113

Here only six accidentals are needed; the flattened notes,

coming *after* the unflattened ones, do not require contradiction. But the sharpened 4th degree (D♮) does have to be contradicted.

11. Follow the steps in this working of a harmonic chromatic scale with the minor signature. We will take the key of F sharp. The scale is first written without accidentals, i.e. just an octave of notes:

Ex. 114

The flattened 2nd is G♮. The sharpened 3rd, 4th, 6th and 7th are respectively A♯, B♯, D♯, and E♯. Insert these in the appropriate spaces and the result is:

Ex. 115

This has six accidentals.
The descending form appears thus:

Ex. 116

This has nine accidentals.

12. The number of accidentals to the octave is a useful check.
With the *major* signature—nine up, six down.
With the *minor* signature—six up, nine down.

13. In chromatic scales written without key-signature the number of accidentals varies, but the method of working is the same as that already given. The first step is to write the *major* scale of the key with the necessary sharps or flats as accidentals. Then insert the extra notes according to the rule given in para. 7 for scales with the major signature. The harmonic chromatic scale of B, without key-signature:
Step 1:

Ex. 117

Step 2:

Ex. 118

The 2nd, 3rd, 6th and 7th degrees are all sharp, so to flatten them they all become natural. But no accidentals are needed for the inserted notes, since they are natural in any case.

The harmonic chromatic scale of G flat, without signature: Step 1:

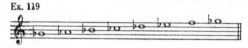

Ex. 119

Step 2:

Ex. 120

Here every single note requires an accidental.

14. The **melodic chromatic scale** is an *ascending form only*; descending it follows the rules for the harmonic form. Ascending it needs fewer accidentals than the harmonic and is therefore easier to read—which is its whole purpose. The rules for construction are:

(i) *With the major key-signature.* Write the scale and add every degree sharpened except 3rd and 7th.

(ii) *With the minor key-signature.* Write the scale *without accidentals*, and add every degree sharpened except 2nd and 5th.

Thus, the melodic chromatic scale of C with the major signature is:

Ex. 121

With the minor signature it is:

Ex. 122

In both cases only five accidentals are needed.

15. A melodic chromatic scale without key-signature is, of course, a theoretical possibility, and the number of accidentals is variable. The first step is to write the major scale with the necessary sharps or flats as accidentals, and then insert the extra notes according to the major key rule given above. For example, the melodic chromatic scale of F sharp, without key-signature:

Ex. 123

This looks fearsome, but is in perfectly correct notation.

16. In writing chromatic scales in notes grouped according to a given time-signature, allow for the fact that an accidental lasts to the end of the bar in which it occurs. For example:

Write one octave, ascending and descending, of the melodic chromatic scale of E with the major key-signature. Write in semiquavers, in $\frac{4}{4}$ time, and complete the final bar with rests in correct order.

The answer is:

Ex. 124

In both cases, the accidental at the end of the first bar. C has already been made double-sharp in the ascending scale, and this has to be contradicted in descending.

Note the accidental at the end of the first bar. C has already been made double-sharp in the ascending scale, and this has to be contradicted in descending.

17. The intelligent student may possibly be inclined to ask, 'Why all this complicated notation? Surely, since the chromatic scale uses up every possible note within the octave, one notation could serve for all keys?'

The answer is that certainly one notation *could* be used for all keys, but the difficulties in reading would in many cases become needlessly great. There is, actually, a perfectly logical reason for the methods of notation explained in this chapter, connected with 'chromatic harmony'. Any explanation of this would be quite incomprehensible to the elementary student, who must be prepared to accept things on trust, at least until his musical knowledge has advanced to the stage where an explanation would be understandable.

QUESTIONS AND EXERCISES ON CHAPTER 10

1. What is a chromatic scale?
2. Explain and give examples of the two kinds of semitone.
3. Explain the derivation of the harmonic chromatic scale.
4. Write, in minims, one ascending octave of each of these harmonic chromatic scales, with major key-signatures:
    G, E flat, B, D flat.
5. Write, in crotchets, one descending octave of each of these harmonic chromatic scales, with major key-signatures:
    D, B flat, C sharp, A flat.
6. Write, in quavers, one octave ascending and descending of each of these harmonic chromatic scales, without key-signatures:
    F, A, G flat, F sharp.
7. Write, in semibreves, one ascending octave of each of these melodic chromatic scales, with major key-signatures:
    B flat, E, G flat, F sharp.
8. Write, in semiquavers, one octave, ascending and descending, of each of these melodic chromatic scales, with minor key-signatures:
    E, F, G sharp, E flat.
9. Above each of these notes write a diatonic semitone:

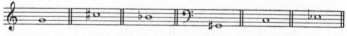

10. Above each of these notes write a chromatic semitone:

11. Write one octave, ascending and descending, of each of these chromatic scales. Group the notes according to the stated time-signatures, inserting barlines, and complete the final bars with rests in proper order:
    G melodic, in quavers, in $\frac{9}{8}$ time
    C sharp harmonic, in demisemiquavers, $\frac{6}{16}$ time
    F sharp melodic, in semiquavers, $\frac{6}{4}$ time

CHAPTER 11

INTERVALS (I)

1. An **interval** is the difference in pitch between two sounds. Intervals are measured in two ways:

   (*a*) Numerically,
   (*b*) According to their quality.

2. The numerical name of an interval depends on the number of letter-names it contains, this being reckoned inclusively. Thus, from C up to E is a 3rd, since the interval covers three letter-names—C, D and E. From G up to D is a 5th, since it covers the five letter-names G, A, B, C, D. Note that this method of reckoning applies whether the notes concerned are ♯, ♭, ♮, or anything else; merely the letter-names are taken into account.

3. The quality of an interval depends actually on the number of semitones it contains, though this fact does not need to be taken into account in reckoning. There are five 'qualifying names' for intervals, namely: perfect, major, minor, augmented, and diminished. Only the unison,[1] 4th, 5th and 8th (or octave) can be termed perfect; they are never major or minor. 2nds, 3rds, 6ths and 7ths may be major or minor, but are never perfect.

4. The standard of measurement for the quality of intervals is the major scale, and the basic rule is:

   The ascending major scale gives the perfect 4th, 5th and octave, and the major 2nd, 3rd, 6th and 7th above its tonic.

   Thus, in the scale of C major, C to D—tonic to second degree of the scale—is a major 2nd; C to E is a major 3rd; C to F—tonic to 4th degree—is a perfect 4th; C to G a perfect 5th; C to A a major 6th; and C to B a major 7th.

[1] A 'unison' ('single sound') occurs when two voices or instruments sound the same note simultaneously.

Ex. 125

5. This rule applies in any scale. The lower note of the interval is taken as the tonic. The 4th, 5th and 8th degrees of the scale are a perfect 4th, 5th and octave above the tonic; the 2nd, 3rd, 6th and 7th degrees are respectively a major 2nd, 3rd, 6th and 7th above it. For example, in E flat major:

Ex. 126

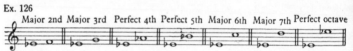

6. To find a major or a perfect interval above a given note, we therefore take this note as the tonic of a major scale and find the appropriate scale-degree. For example, a major 6th above B is the 6th note of the scale of B major, i.e. G sharp. A perfect 5th above A flat is the 5th note of the scale of A flat major, i.e. E flat.

Ex. 127

7. A minor interval is a chromatic semitone smaller than the corresponding major one. Note that in changing the quality of an interval *the letter-names must must not be altered.* Thus, a major 3rd above C is E (see ex. 125), so the minor 3rd is E♭. The major 6th above B is G♯ (see ex. 127), so the minor 6th is G♮.

Ex. 128

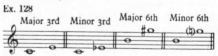

To find a minor interval above a given note, first find the major one and then lower the upper note a chromatic semitone.

8. A diminished interval is a chromatic semitone smaller than a minor or a perfect one. The minor 3rd above C is E♭

(ex. 128), so the diminished 3rd will be E♭♭. The E♭ is lowered a chromatic semitone.

Ex. 129

(Let it again be stressed that letter-names may not be changed. E♭♭ is enharmonically D♮, but to write D instead of E♭♭ would change the number of the interval. C to D is a second, not a third.)

A perfect 5th above C is G, so a diminished 5th is G♭.

Ex. 130

Similarly with any other given notes.

9. Suppose we have to find a diminished 4th above D. The perfect 4th is the 4th note of the scale of D major—G. The diminished 4th is a semitone smaller, so we lower the G a chromatic semitone. Hence:

Ex. 131

Diminished 4th

Suppose we have to find a diminished 7th above A. The major 7th is the 7th note of the major scale—G♯. The minor 7th is therefore G♮, one semitone lower, and the diminished 7th a chromatic semitone lower still—G♭.

Ex. 132 Major 7th   Minor 7th   Diminished 7th

10. An augmented interval is a chromatic semitone larger than a major or a perfect one. Thus, the major 2nd above B flat is C, second note of the major scale; so the augmented 2nd must be C♯.

Ex. 133

Major 2nd   Augmented 2nd

Similarly, the augmented 5th above B♭ is the fifth note of the major scale (F, the perfect 5th) raised a chromatic semitone, i.e. F♯.

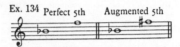

Ex. 134 Perfect 5th   Augmented 5th

11. To identify a given interval, take the lower note as a tonic. Count up the number of letter-names included to find the numerical name. Then decide whether the pitch of the upper note is the same as it would be in the major scale of the lower note, or whether it has been raised or lowered. For example:

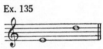

Ex. 135

Any kind of E up to any kind of D is a 7th. In the scale of E major, D is sharp and this would be the major 7th. The given note is natural, i.e. a chromatic semitone lower than D♯. So the given interval is a minor 7th.
Again:

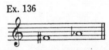

Ex. 136

F to A is a 3rd of some kind. The third note of F♯ major is A♯—the major 3rd. A♭ is A♯ lowered *two* chromatic semitones, so the interval is a diminished 3rd.
And again:

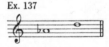

Ex. 137

A to D is a 4th. The 4th note of A♭ major is D♭, the perfect 4th. D♮ is a semitone above D♭, so the interval is an augmented 4th.

12. Sometimes the lower note, owing to accidentals, cannot be taken as the tonic of a scale. Suppose we have to write a diminished 7th above D♯. There is no such thing in

notation as the scale of D♯ major. *Do not convert the D♯
into E♭.* The method is to take away the ♯, giving D♮,
a manageable tonic. Find the diminished 7th above D♮
and then raise both notes a chromatic semitone, thus:

Ex. 138.

13. The same method applies in identifying intervals in which
the lower note is not a manageable tonic, for example:

Ex. 139

It is obviously a 5th of some kind, but F × is no use as a
tonic. Lower both notes a chromatic semitone, giving:

Ex. 140

This is identified as a diminished 5th, which is therefore
the correct description of our original interval.

14. To find an interval *below* a given note the basic rule is:

The descending major scale gives the perfect 4th, 5th
and octave, and the *minor* 2nd, 3rd, 6th and 7th below
the tonic.

Thus, in C major:

Ex. 141

The other qualities of intervals are found by chromatically
altering the *lower* note. A major interval is a chromatic
semitone larger than a minor one, so the lower note of the
minor would be dropped a chromatic semitone. A diminished interval is a chromatic semitone smaller than a
perfect one, so the lower note would be raised a chromatic
semitone. Examples will make this clear.

(i) Write a major 6th below A♭.

The 6th note down the scale of A♭ major is C, the *minor* 6th. For the major 6th this C must be shifted a semitone farther away from the A♭, i.e. C♭.

Ex. 142

If we were asked to give the augmented 6th below, then the C would be moved yet another semitone farther from the A♭, i.e. C♭♭.

Ex. 143

(ii) Write a diminished 5th below F♯.

The 5th note down the scale of F♯ major is B, the perfect 5th. For the diminished interval this B must be brought a semitone nearer to the F♯, i.e. B♯.

Ex. 144

15. A **harmonic** interval is one in which the two notes are sounded together (ex. 145 (*a*)). In a **melodic** interval they are sounded one after the other (ex. 145 (*b*)).

Ex. 145

QUESTIONS AND EXERCISES ON CHAPTER 11

1. What is an interval? How are intervals measured?
2. What are the 'qualifying names' applied to intervals? Which intervals are never called perfect?
3. Give the basic rule for the measurement of the quality of an interval above a given note.
4. What is the difference between a major interval and a minor one?

5. What is the difference between (a) a minor interval and a diminished one, (b) a perfect interval and a diminished one?

6. What is the difference between a major or a perfect interval and an augmented one?

7. Name these intervals:

8. Above each of these notes write the interval required:

9. Give the basic rule for the measurement of the quality of an interval below a given note.

10. Below each of these notes write the interval required:

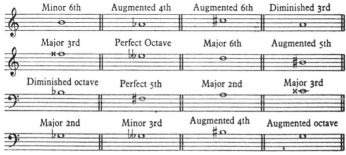

11. Distinguish between a harmonic interval and a melodic one.

CHAPTER 12

INTERVALS (II)

1. Intervals are classified as **concords** or **discords**. A **concord** is a combination of sounds which is satisfactory in itself and needs nothing to follow it. A **discord** is not satisfactory in itself and needs to be followed by some more satisfactory combination which is called its **resolution.** Resolution is defined as 'passing from a discord to a concord'. For example:

Ex. 146

is satisfactory. We do not feel, as it were, left hanging in mid-air. On the other hand:

Ex. 147

leaves a feeling of unrest. It wants to resolve:

Ex. 148

2. Concords are of two kinds, perfect and imperfect. The perfect concords are the perfect unison, 4th, 5th and octave; the imperfect concords are the major and minor 3rd and 6th. All other intervals—whatever they may sound like when played in isolation—are discords. So that *all 2nds and 7ths, and all augmented and diminished intervals are discords.*

3. An interval may be **inverted**, that is, turned upside-down, by putting the upper note an octave lower, or the lower note an octave higher, so that their positions are reversed. Thus,

Ex. 149

inverts into

Ex. 150

The numerical size and the quality of an interval are changed by inversion. To find the number of the inverted interval, subtract the original one from 9. A 5th becomes a 4th (see ex. 150), a 3rd becomes a 6th, and so on. With regard to quality:

Major becomes minor
Minor becomes major
Augmented becomes diminished
Diminished becomes augmented
Perfect *remains* perfect

The diminished 5th in ex. 149 inverts into an augmented 4th. Similarly, a minor 7th inverts into a major 2nd; and so on.

4. Every major or minor scale contains seven of every numerical interval—seven 2nds, seven 3rds, etc.—since one of each may be built on each degree of the scale. Ex. 151 makes this clear. Note that the scale is not limited to one octave.

Ex. 151

And so on for 5ths, 6ths and 7ths.

F

5. Intervals are classified as **diatonic** or **chromatic.** (We have already noted this in connection with semitones.) Diatonic intervals occur between degrees of the diatonic scales (i.e. major and minor scales), in the manner shown in ex. 151. They also, of course, occur in the chromatic scale. Chromatic intervals are found in the chromatic scale only.

The chromatic intervals are:

(i) The chromatic semitone (or 'augmented unison') and its inversion the diminished octave.

(ii) The augmented 3rd and its inversion the diminished 6th.

(iii) The augmented 6th and its inversion the diminished 3rd.

Chromatic semitones in a chromatic scale are sufficiently numerous to need no tabulation.

The augmented 3rd occurs on the flattened second degree of the harmonic chromatic scale; its inversion, the diminished 6th, occurs on the sharpened fourth degree. Thus, in C harmonic chromatic:

Ex. 152

An **augmented 6th** occurs on the flattened second and flattened sixth degrees of the harmonic chromatic scale, and a diminished 3rd on its sharpened 4th and 7th degrees:

Ex. 153

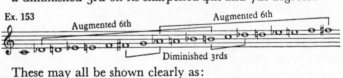

These may all be shown clearly as:

Ex. 154

6. Intervals are also classified as **simple** or **compound.** A simple interval is one which does not exceed the compass of an octave, and all the intervals so far dealt with

are simple ones. A compound interval is greater than an octave. To find the compound form of a simple interval, add 7 to its number. Thus:

Ex. 155

is a major 2nd;

Ex. 156

is a major 9th. It may also be described as a compound major 2nd. Similarly, a 10th is a compound 3rd, an 11th is a compound 4th, and so on.

Ex. 157

Minor 3rd Minor 10th Perfect 4th Perfect 11th

7. In inverting a compound interval remember that what was originally the upper note must become the lower one, and vice versa. This means that one of them must be shifted *two* octaves, e.g.:

Ex. 158

inverts into:

Ex. 159   or

If, for example, we merely lower the upper note one octave, we have:

Ex. 160

in which the A is still above the E; the interval is not inverted.

8. Most intervals occur in more than one key. For example, the augmented 4th:

Ex. 161.

occurs in all the scales which contain a C♯ but not a G♯, i.e.

Ex. 162

9. To find all the keys in which a given interval occurs, consider its sharps or flats and decide what key-signature or signatures they can imply. For example:

Ex. 163

Since this contains a D♭, the key-signature cannot have fewer than four flats. This gives A♭ major and F Minor. But B♭ and D♭ also occur in the signatures with five, six and seven flats. The five-flat keys, D♭ major and B♭ minor, both contain the the given interval. Of the six-flat keys, G♭ major contains it, but E♭ minor does not, because of its sharpened leading-note, D♮. The seven-flat keys are C♭ major and A♭ minor, both of which contain the given interval. The complete list is therefore:

A♭ major, F minor, D♭ major, B♭ minor, G♭ major, C♭ major and A♭ minor.

10. In dealing with this kind of question—common enough in some examination papers—always remember to allow for the sharpened leading-note in the minor key. For example:

Ex. 164

may appear puzzling—there is no key-signature which contains both sharps and flats. But the one-flat minor key —D—has C♯ for its leading-note, and this is the key of this interval.

11. Remember that as scale-degrees, double-sharps only occur as minor-key leading notes (see the table of minor scales in Chap. 9). So, for example,

Ex. 165

can only occur in the harmonic minor scale in which F × is the leading-note, that is, G sharp minor.

12. Remember, too, that the leading-notes of all flat minor keys except D and G are ♮. For example:

Ex. 166

If the key-signature is to contain a G♭ it must also contain an A♭. This would give D♭ major or B♭ minor. D♭ major is impossible because of the A♮, but this note is the leading-note of B♭ minor, which is the key of the interval.

13. The name of an interval may be changed by altering one of its notes enharmonically (see Chap. 7). Thus, in ex. 167 (*a*) can be changed to (*b*):

Ex. 167

(*b*) is called the **enharmonic equivalent** of (*a*).

To find the enharmonic equivalent of a given interval, only *one* of its notes should be altered—the note which is 'farthest away from C major'. An example will make this clear. Give the enharmonic equivalent of this interval:

Ex. 168

F♯ is the first sharp to occur in a key-signature; it is only one remove from C major. D♯ is the fourth sharp to occur in a key-signature, and so is 'farther away from C major' than is F♯. D♯ is therefore changed to E♭.

Ex. 169

If we retain the D♯ and change the F♯ to G♭ we have:

Ex. 170

which could be described as a doubly-augmented 5th—a somewhat improbable affair!

If both notes are ♮ it does not matter which is changed:

Ex. 171

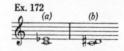

In both cases the minor 7th becomes an augmented 6th.

14. By enharmonic change a discord may become a concord and vice versa. Ex. 172 (*a*) is a minor 3rd, an imperfect concord; (*b*) is an augmented 2nd, a discord.

Ex. 172

The apparent oddity that the same two sounds can be either a concord or a discord, according to the way in which they are written, has a perfectly logical explanation. This, however, would be far beyond the student's understanding at this stage, and must be taken on trust.

15. When the two notes of an interval are on two different staves, remember that the link between the treble and the

bass is middle C. The notes concerned must be considered in their relation to this pivotal note. For example, to write a diminished 5th below the given note, on the bass stave:

Ex. 173

The given E is the one immediately above middle C, so a diminished 5th below it will be the A♯ immediately below it, i.e. ex. 174 (*a*). Transferred to the bass, this gives ex. 174 (*b*).

Ex. 174

It is all too common to find notes written an octave too high or too low in such cases.

QUESTIONS AND EXERCISES ON CHAPTER 12

1. Define concord, discord and resolution.
2. Which intervals are (*a*) perfect concords, (*b*) imperfect concords?
3. What is meant by inverting an interval?
4. Write the inversion of each of these intervals, and below each inversion state its name. State also whether each interval is concord (perfect or imperfect) or discord:

5. (*a*) Write out all the 6ths contained in the scale of E major, naming each as major or minor.
   (*b*) Write out all the 4ths contained in the scale of F harmonic minor, naming each as perfect, augmented or diminished.
6. Distinguish between diatonic and chromatic intervals, naming those which are chromatic.
7. Write out the augmented 3rd and the two augmented 6ths which occur in each of these harmonic chromatic scales:
   G, E flat, B, D flat.

8. Write out the diminished 6th and the two diminished 3rds which occur in each of these harmonic chromatic scales:
   F, E, A flat, F sharp.

9. What is the difference between a simple and a compound interval?

10. Name these intervals and give the inversion of each:

11. Name all the keys in which each of the following intervals occurs:

12. Write the following intervals, and after each write and name its enharmonic equivalent:
    Augmented 4th above G
    Diminished 3rd below A flat
    Augmented 5th above D sharp
    Minor 7th below G sharp
    Diminished octave above D
    Chromatic semitone below F sharp

13. On each vacant section of stave write the required interval. Mark each interval as perfect concord (P.), imperfect concord (I.), or discord (D.):

Minor 6th above	Minor 13th below	Diminished 11th above	Major 7th below

Perfect 5th above	Augmented 6th below	Augmented 4th above	Diminished 3rd below

14. In the following passage name all the intervals marked ⌐￢. Describe each as (*a*) simple or compound, (*b*) perfect or imperfect concord, or discord, (*c*) diatonic or chromatic.

CHAPTER 13

TRANSPOSITION

1. To transpose a piece of music means to sound it, or to write it, at a different pitch from that at which it is originally given.

2. Written transposition is best made clear by working examples.

Transpose this melody up an octave:

Ex. 175

After inserting the clef, key-signature and time-signature on the new stave, find the note one octave above the first note of the given passage, thus:

Ex. 176

From this, follow the rise and fall of the given melody, i.e. from F up a step to G, down a 3rd to E, up a 4th to A, and so on. All that has to be watched is the direction of the stems in the new version. Hence:

Ex. 177

Exactly the same method should be followed in transposing down an octave without change of clef.

3. Now suppose we have to transpose the same passage down an octave into the bass stave. Middle C, the link between the two staves, is our guide. The first note, F, is the first F above middle C. One octave below it is therefore the first F *below* middle C, i.e.:

Ex. 178

From this point proceed as explained in para. 2, and the result is:

Ex. 179

4. Transpose this melody into the treble stave, *at the same pitch*:

Ex. 180

Middle C is again our guide. The first note is the F immediately above middle C. In the treble this is:

Ex. 181

Working as explained in para. 2, the result is:

Ex. 182

5. All this is so simple that it is hardly possible to go wrong. Transposition to a new key brings a little complication. Transpose this melody up an augmented 2nd, inserting the new key-signature:

Ex. 183

The first step is to find the new key-signature, and in this connection it is *not* necessary to decide whether the given passage is in a major key or in its relative minor. Assume it to be in the major key indicated by the signature—the result will be the same in any case. Ex. 183 has three flats, the signature of E flat major. An augmented 2nd above E flat is F sharp, giving us a new signature of six sharps. This, with the time-signature, is now written:

Ex. 184

Now transpose each note up a 2nd, working by letter-names only and *disregarding all accidentals*. A 2nd above E is F, a 2nd above F is G, a 2nd above A is B, and so on. Hence:

Ex. 185

We now have to deal with the accidentals. For each accidental in the original there must be a corresponding one in the transposed version. Each of these new accidentals will have the same effect as the corresponding one in the original, but it will not necessarily be the same accidental, since we have to allow for the new key-signature. Each accidentalised note in ex. 183 must be compared with the signature to find the effect of its accidental. The accidentals have been numbered for reference.

1. In the signature, E is ♭, so the ♮ raises it a semitone. To raise the corresponding note a semitone in ex. 185 we must use a ✕.

2. In the signature there is no reference to F, so it is therefore ♮. The ♯ raises it a semitone. In ex. 185 the corresponding G is ♯, so must become ✕.

3. This ♮ actually contradicts the preceding F♯. *Do not think of it this way*, but compare it with the signature. According to the signature, F is ♮, so the ♮ sign *restores it to its key-signature pitch*. In the signature of ex. 185 G is ♯, so a ♯ must be placed before the note concerned.

4. This is similar to 3; the E in ex. 183 is restored to its key-signature pitch. In ex. 185 the corresponding F must therefore have a ♯.

5. The ♭ lowers the note a semitone. In ex. 185 the E is ♯; lowered a semitone it becomes ♮.

6. The ♮ raises the key-signature B♭ a semitone. The corresponding C♯ in ex. 185 therefore needs a ✕.

7. The ♮ restores the D to its key-signature pitch, so in ex. 185 the corresponding E needs a ♯. Hence:

Ex. 186

6. The above, admittedly, may seem rather involved and long-winded. If it is properly understood and digested error in transposition should be impossible.

7. In transposition from one clef to another, all that has to be remembered is the importance of middle C as the link between treble and bass.

Transpose the following down a major 6th into the bass stave:

Ex. 187

The two-sharp signature indicates D major. A major 6th below D is F, key-signature one flat:

Ex. 188

The first note is the F above middle C. A 6th below it is the A below middle C, which in the bass is:

Ex. 189

Now transpose by letter-names only, as already explained, and then deal with the accidentals. The solution is:

Ex. 190

8. A transposition question may not state the interval which the passage is to be transposed, but may instead state the key.

Transpose the following up into the key of G minor:

Ex. 191

Since the new key is stated to be minor, that of the original must also be minor. The four-sharp signature gives C sharp minor. G, the new tonic, is a diminished 5th above C sharp. Find the new signature—two flats—and proceed as already explained, i.e. put each note up five letter-names and then deal with the accidentals. Hence:

Ex. 192

QUESTIONS AND EXERCISES ON CHAPTER 13

1. Transpose these passages up one octave without change of clef.

2. Transpose these passages down one octave without change of clef.

3. Transpose these passages up one octave into the treble stave.

4. Transpose these passages down one octave into the bass stave.

5. Transpose (*a*) into the bass stave, at the same pitch; and (*b*) into the treble stave at the same pitch.

6. Transpose the following as directed, without change of clef.

(*a*) Up a minor 3rd:

(*b*) Down a diminished 5th:

(*c*) Down an augmented 4th:

(*d*) Up a major 6th:

(e) Up a minor 7th:

(f) Down a major 2nd:

7. Transpose the following as directed.

(a) Up a perfect 4th into the treble stave:

(b) Down a diminished 7th into the bass stave:

8. Transpose the following as directed.

(a) Up into F major:

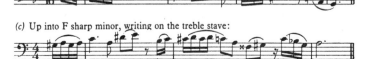

(b) Down into B minor:

(c) Up into F sharp minor, writing on the treble stave:

CHAPTER 14

THE C CLEF. SHORT AND OPEN SCORE

1. Besides the G and F clefs already dealt with, there is also a third clef—C. It was formerly much employed, but is now very restricted in its uses. It is written in two shapes:

       or

For manuscript writing the former is the better as it is easier to form it clearly.

2. The **C clef** is always placed 'on a line', that is, a line passes through it as shown above. This line is *middle C*. Nowadays the clef may be used on either the third or the fourth line of the stave. On the third line it was formerly used for the alto voice and is therefore generally known as the **alto clef**; on the fourth line it was for the tenor voice, and so known as the **tenor clef**. These names are not strictly accurate; its proper name is C clef. But it is obviously less cumbersome to refer to 'the alto clef' than to 'the C clef on the third line of the stave'.

Ex. 193

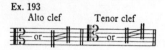

Alto clef   Tenor clef

3. Other positions of the C clef, now disused, were:

Ex. 194

(a) is the **soprano clef**, (b) the **mezzo-soprano clef.**

4. The reason for the use of these various positions of the clef was to avoid leger lines. The average compasses of the alto and tenor voices, for example, are:

Ex. 195

which, in the treble and bass clefs respectively, involve two or three such leger lines for the extreme notes. In the C clef these are:

Ex. 196 Alto   Tenor

Only one leger line is needed in each case.

5. The only present-day uses of the C clefs are:

(a)

for the viola, changing to the G clef for high passages which would involve many leger lines; and:

(b)

for higher notes on the tenor trombone, the 'cello and the bassoon.

6. Ex. 197 shows the placing of sharps and flats in key-signatures in the C clefs. Note that in the tenor the F sharp is *below* the C sharp, unlike its position in all other clefs. It is *not* placed above the top line of the stave.

Ex. 197

7. In transposing a passage from the G or F clef to the C clef, middle C is the guiding note, as explained in Chap. 13.

8. A **'score'** is a set of two or more staves with the clefs appropriate to the voices or instruments concerned in the performance.

9. **Pianoforte score,** or **'short score',** consists of two staves connected by a **'brace'** {. The clefs are normally 𝄞 for the upper stave and 𝄢 for the lower, according to the pitch of the music.

N.B. Avoid the elementary error of referring to the 𝄞 as

G

the 'right-hand clef', and the ☉: as the 'left-hand clef'. In piano music the right hand may quite frequently descend into the bass register, or the left hand rise into the treble register.

10. The greater amount of choral music, that is, music for a choir, is written for four voices or 'parts'. The highest is the soprano (or treble), the next highest the alto; then the tenor and, lowest of all, the bass. These names are often abbreviated to the letters S.A.T.B. respectively. In short score the S. and A. are written on the upper stave, with the treble clef, and the T. and B. on the lower, with the bass clef. S. and T. have their stems upwards, A. and B. downwards, thus:

Ex. 198

When two parts on the same stave coincide on the same note, that note must have both an up and a down stem, unless it is a semibreve, in which case two notes must be written, side by side.

Ex. 199

11. If what is normally a lower part rises above what is normally a higher one (or a normally higher one passes below a lower one) the parts are said to cross. When this crossing of parts is between two parts on the same stave, i.e. between S. and A., or between T. and B., the direction of the stems makes their movement clear.

Ex. 200

From the second beat the soprano lies below the alto. Soprano stems remain upwards, alto ones downwards. The soprano line is shown at (*a*) below, the alto at (*b*).

Ex. 201

12. When a separate stave is used for each voice or instrument we have **open score**. Open score for S.A.T.B. is called **vocal score** and exists in two forms. The older form is now only to be found in old editions of vocal music (and in certain examination papers), and uses four clefs— G, C alto, C tenor and F.

Ex. 202

In examination papers this is described as 'vocal score with the proper C clefs for the alto and tenor'.

Modern vocal score employs the G clef for the S., A. and T., and the F clef for the B. The tenor notes are written one octave above their actual pitch. Many modern editions of vocal music indicate this by a small 8 below the

G clef—♵. Another system is to use the 'double G clef'

for the tenor—♵♵. But neither of these is really needed, since it has for long been conventional to understand that a tenor part written in the G clef is to sound an octave below its written pitch.

'Vocal score with G clefs for the S., A. and T.' therefore appears thus:

Ex. 203

13. A **string quartet** consists of 1st violin, 2nd violin, viola and violoncello. The two violins use the G clef, the viola the C alto, and the 'cello the F clef, unless, of course, either of the two last rises high enough to warrant a change of clef. The score is:

Ex. 204

14. In any kind of open score the direction of the stems of the notes depends entirely on their position on the stave, as explained in Chap. 3.

15. In transferring a passage from short score to open score three points need especial care:

    (i) Crossing of parts;
    (ii) Transference from one clef to another;
    (iii) Accidentals.

    (i) is dealt with in para. 11, (ii) in para 7.

16. With regard to accidentals, it must be remembered that

in short score a single accidental may affect notes in two different parts on the same stave, e.g.:

Ex. 205

The sharp to the initial F in the upper part affects also the F (third quaver) in the lower part. An accidental cannot affect a note on another stave, so that if this passage is written out in open score a separate sharp must be provided for the F in the lower part, i.e.:

Ex. 206

This is the only real trap in transference from short to open score. To avoid falling into it, take each accidental in turn and follow it along its own line or space to the end of the bar, and see whether it affects a note in another part.

17. Note also the case of the accidental which is needed in short score but not in open score.

Ex. 207 (a) (b)

No ♮ is needed for the F at *, since being on another stave it is not affected by the ♯ at the beginning of the bar.

18. Ex. 208 sums up all the above. (a) is the short score version; (b), (c) and (d) show it rewritten in 'vocal score with G clefs', 'vocal score with C clefs' and 'open score for string quartet' respectively.

Ex. 208

In the short score version note the placing of the **rests**. The rules given in Chap. 4 must perforce be disregarded for the sake of clarity.

19. In rewriting a passage in open score and at the same time transposing it to another key, each part should be dealt with separately. After inserting clefs, new key-signature, and time-signature, transpose the parts one at a time, and pay particular attention to para. 16 above.

20. An **orchestral score** or **full score** has a separate stave for each instrument or group of instruments, and according to the size of the orchestra employed may need up to thirty or more staves for each line of music. The German term is **partitur**; the French is **partition.**

QUESTIONS AND EXERCISES ON CHAPTER 14

1. Which note is indicated by the C clef? On a stave show this clef in its alto and tenor positions.
   What are the present-day uses of the C clef?
2. Write the key-signatures of these keys in (*a*) the alto clef, and (*b*) the tenor clef:
   D major, F minor, B flat minor, G sharp minor, F sharp minor, E flat major
3. Rewrite these passages at the same pitch in the alto clef:

4. Rewrite these passages at the same pitch in the tenor clef:

5. Rewrite these passages (*a*) at the same pitch in the alto clef, and (*b*) at the same pitch in the tenor clef.

(a)

(b)

6. Transpose these passages as directed:

(a) Down a major 3rd into the alto clef:

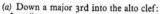

(b) Up an augmented 4th into the tenor clef:

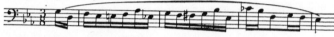

(c) Down a diminished 3rd into the treble clef:

(d) Up a minor 3rd into the bass clef:

7. Explain what is meant by short score.
8. Explain what is meant by open score.
9. Set out the clefs for:
    (a) vocal score with C clefs for the alto and tenor
    (b) modern vocal score
    (c) open score for string quartet
10. Rewrite this passage at the same pitch,
    (a) in vocal score with C clefs for the alto and tenor
    (b) in modern vocal score
    (c) in open score for string quartet

11. Rewrite this passage at the same pitch in short score:

12. Transpose the following passages as directed:

(a) Up a semitone into vocal score with G clefs for alto and tenor:

(b) Down a diminished 3rd into open score for string quartet:

(c) Up into the key of G minor, in open score with C clefs for alto and tenor:

CHAPTER 15

SIGNS AND ABBREVIATIONS

1. The sign ⌒ or ⌣ is called a **pause** or **fermata**, and is placed over or under a note or chord. It indicates that the note or chord is to be held as long as the performer pleases. The Italian word is *pausa*.

Ex. 209

2. The letters G.P. abbreviate the German word *general-pause*, indicating a pause for the whole orchestra. Found in orchestral scores.

3. The letters L.P. abbreviate the Italian *lunga pausa*, long pause. They imply a pause of unusual length.

4. Signs indicating accent or stress are > and ∧, placed over or under single notes or chords.

Ex. 210

Note that in performance the strength of an accent must depend on the surrounding degree of tone of the passage as a whole. An accent in a soft passage is obviously by no means as marked as one in a loud passage.

5. A **slur** is a curved line placed over or under a passage. It is not to be confused with a tie. A tie joins two notes of the same pitch, and the first of these must be long enough to last until the second one is due. A slur covers two or more notes, not of the same pitch, and indicates that they are to be played smoothly. Note the Italian term for smoothly—*legato*.

Ex. 211

6. The Italian word *staccato* means short or detached. (Note the correct spelling—a double c, but *no double t*.)   There are three degrees of *staccato*:

> (*a*) Simple *staccato*—short—indicated by dots over or under the notes concerned—Ex. 212 (*a*).
> (*b*) *Staccatissimo*—very short—indicated by dashes over or under the notes—Ex. 212 (*b*).
> (*c*) *Mezzo staccato*—half short—indicated by dots combined with slurs—Ex. 212 (*c*).

(*a*) shortens each note by approximately a half; (*b*) shortens each note by approximately three-quarters; (*c*) shortens each note by approximately one quarter.   In each case the full value of the note must be made up by rests.   These shortenings are, as stated, only approximate; the actual interpretation must depend ultimately on the style of the piece concerned.

Ex. 212

A single note to be played *mezzo staccato* is shown by a dot and a line—see ex. 212 (*d*).

7. A horizontal line over or under a note indicates *tenuto*—held or sustained.   It is a warning to be sure to give the note its full value, and generally also implies some degree of stress.

Ex. 213

8. A passage to be repeated is enclosed between double bar-lines, dots being placed after the first and in front of the second:

Ex. 214

This is played as:

Ex. 215

Sometimes four dots are used:

Ex. 216

9. If the passage to be repeated starts at the beginning of a piece, the double bar and dots need only be placed at its end.

Ex. 217

Written

Played

10. Sometimes a passage is to be repeated but with a different continuation the second time. In this case the terms *prima volta* and *seconda volta* (first time and second time) are used. They are normally abbreviated to *1ma volta* and *2da volta*, or even to a mere 1 and 2, thus:

Ex. 218

Written

Played

11. D.S. or D.$. abbreviates the Italian *dal segno*, 'from the sign'. A return is to be made from the point where the sign $ appears in the music. More often, *D.S. al fine* is used. *Fine* is the Italian for end or finish, so *D.$. al fine*

means 'return to the sign *$* and play as far as the word *fine*.'

12. D.C. abbreviates *da capo*, 'from the beginning'. *Da capo al fine* therefore means 'return to the beginning and play as far as the word *fine*'.

13. In many eighteenth-century works *menuetto da capo*, or simply M.D.C., is found. As a rule a minuet (a kind of dance) was followed by a second minuet, usually known as a trio, and after this trio the original minuet was repeated, this repetition being indicated by M.D.C. Similarly with the scherzo, a more playful movement which gradually replaced the minuet as the third movement of a symphony or sonata. Like the minuet, the scherzo normally had a trio, and at the end of this trio the words *scherzo D.C.* might appear.

14. Rather rarely the word *bis* (Latin for twice) may be found over a passage, indicating that it is to be immediately repeated:

15. Repetition of a single bar, or of a passage within a single bar, may be shown by one of these signs:

Thus:

This method is confined to orchestral music.

16. A single note to be divided into repeated quavers may have a thick stroke through its stem, representing the quaver's tail. If the note be a semibreve, the stroke will be above or below it.

Ex. 221

Similarly, division into repeated semiquavers will be shown by two such strokes through the stem, into demisemiquavers by three, and so on. If the original note is itself a quaver, repetition in semiquavers is shown by one stroke, in demisemiquavers by two, and so on:

Ex. 222

17. The rapid alternation of two notes of different pitch is shown as below. The value of the alternating notes is indicated by the number of strokes, corresponding to the number of tails. (*a*), with two strokes, indicates alternation in semiquavers; (*b*), with one stroke, in quavers; (*c*), with three strokes, in demisemiquavers.

Ex. 223

In all these, note that in the abbreviated form *both* notes are written in the total value of the written-out version. At (*a*) we have to alternate F and A in semiquavers to the total value of a minim, so both the F and the A are written as minims. Similarly for the other examples.

1. Give the signs for a pause, an accent and a slur.
2. Write out the following as it would (approximately) be performed:

3. Write out the following in full:

4. Explain the abbreviations D.S. and D.C.
5. Write out the following in full:

6. Write out the following in full:

7. Write out the following in full:

CHAPTER 16

ITALIAN TERMS

1. Directions to the performer as to speed, intensity and other matters are usually given in Italian. The custom of employing this language grew up during the seventeenth and eighteenth centuries, and although of late years various composers have tended to give such directions in their own language, Italian is still the most commonly used.

2. **Intensity.** The different degrees and gradations of tone are usually indicated by abbreviations of the full Italian words. The two basic terms are *piano* (*p*), meaning soft, and *forte* (*f*), meaning loud. The ending *-issimo* means very; *mezzo* means half or moderately. From the softest to the loudest degrees of tone we therefore have:

> *Pianissimo* (*pp* or *ppp*)—very soft
> *Piano* (*p*)—soft
> *Mezzo piano* (*mp*)—moderately soft
> *Mezzo forte* (*mf*)—moderately loud
> *Forte* (*f*)—loud
> *Fortissimo* (*ff* or *fff*)—very loud

Medium tone, i.e. neither very soft nor very loud, is sometimes shown by *mv*—*mezza voce*, literally 'half voice'.

3. **Gradual Increase and Decrease of Tone**
> *Crescendo* (*cres.*, *cresc.* or ⟋)—gradually increasing the tone, i.e. becoming louder
> *Decrescendo* (*decres.*)
> *Diminuendo* (*dim.*, *dimin.* or ⟍) } — decreasing or diminishing the tone, i.e. becoming softer

Less common are:

> *Diluendo, morendo*—dying away
> *Scemando*—diminishing in power
> *Smorzando.* (*smorz.*)—dying away

4. **Sudden Increase and Decrease of Tone**
> *Più forte*—more loudly (*più* means more)

Forzando (*fz*), *sforzando* (*sf* or *sfz*)—forcing the tone,
   applied to single notes or chords
Rinforzando (*rf* or *rfz*)—strengthening the tone
Meno forte—less loud (*meno* means less)
Più piano—more softly

The effect of all these, like that of accents, depends on the
surrounding degree of tone. If the passage is *piano*, *sf* or
fz will mean a far smaller accent than if it is *forte*.

5. **Speed (Tempo).** The speed indication is placed above
the stave at the beginning of the first line of a piece.

Grave—very slow indeed, solemn
Lento—slow
Larghissimo—very broadly
Largo—broadly
Larghetto—rather broadly
Adagissimo—very leisurely
Adagio—leisurely
Andante—going at an easy pace
Andantino—at a moderate speed, moving along[1]
Moderato—at moderate speed
Allegretto—fairly fast
Allegro—fast
Vivace—lively
Vivacissimo—very lively
Presto—very quick
Prestissimo—as fast as possible

Note. (i) *Andante* does *not* mean slowly—a common error.
   It is the present participle of the verb *andare*, to go, so
   its literal meaning is 'going', that is, moving along.
(ii) *Allegro* is sometimes given as 'quick, merry, gay'. Strictly
   speaking, its meaning is cheerful or merry, but musically
   it has come simply to mean fast. The third movement
   of Beethoven's 5th symphony is marked *allegro*. It is
   certainly fast, but is hardly merry.

Some of the above may be preceded by *poco*, meaning a
little, or rather. *Poco adagio*—rather leisurely; *poco allegro*—
rather fast.

[1] *Andantino* is sometimes taken to mean slower than *Andante*; opinions
differ.

H

Less common are:
  Celere—nimble
  Tosto—rapid
  Veloce—swiftly

6. **Increase or Decrease of Speed**

  Accelerando (*accel.*)—accelerating, getting gradually faster
  Affrettando—hurrying
  Calcando—hurrying
  Stringendo—pressing onwards, hurrying
  Allargando (*allarg.*)—broadening
  Rallentando (*rall.*)—getting gradually slower
  Ritardando (*rit.*, *ritard.*)—getting gradually slower
  Ritenuto (*rit.*, *riten.*)—held back
  Slargando (*slarg.*)—broadening
  Slentando (*slent.*)—getting slower
  Più mosso—quicker at once
  Più allegro⎫
  Più presto⎬—faster
  Meno mosso—slower at once
  Meno allegro—less fast, slower
  Più lento—more slowly

7. **Speed and Tone Combined**

  Incalzando—getting quicker and louder
  Calando—getting slower and softer
  Morendo—dying away and becoming slower
  Perdendosi—losing itself, i.e. dying away and becoming slower

8. **Other Terms Connected with Speed**

  Ad libitum (*ad lib.*)—at the performer's pleasure as regards the speed
  A piacere—at the performer's pleasure as regards the speed
  A tempo—in time, i.e. return to the original speed after some alteration of it
  Doppio tempo, *doppio movimento*—at twice the speed of the preceding movement or passage
  L'istesso tempo—at the same speed as the preceding movement or passage
  Rubato—robbed, e.g. *tempo rubato*—robbed time, indicating a flexibility in the speed of the beats, though this must not be allowed to destroy or distort the basic rhythm

Tempo commodo—at a comfortable speed

Tempo giusto—in strict or exact time

Tempo ordinario—ordinary speed, i.e. neither too fast nor too slow

Tempo primo—first speed, i.e. return to the first speed after some alteration

9. All the above speed indications are flexible in their interpretation, depending on the style of the music. An exact speed is sometimes shown by the use of a **metronome mark.** The metronome was invented by J. N. Maelzel. It is a clockwork instrument in which a pendulum is fixed at the bottom, instead of at the top as in a clock. Each swing of this pendulum produces a tick. On the pendulum is a sliding weight and behind it a scale marked in figures. The pendulum ticks so many times in a minute according to the figure to which the top of the sliding weight is set. If the weight is set opposite the figure 60, there will be 60 ticks to the minute, and so on. A metronome mark shows how the weight is to be set and the time value of each resulting tick. Thus, ♩=60, means 60 crotchets in a minute; ♩=72, means 72 minims in a minute.

10. A complete list of Italian terms used would need a pocket dictionary. The following only includes the more common ones, such as should be known by an elementary student.

Agitato—agitated

Animato—animated

Appassionato—impassioned

Arco—bow (of a violin, etc.)

Assai—sufficiently, very, e.g. *allegro assai*—very fast

Attacca—go on immediately (to next section of the piece)

Ben—well, e.g. *ben marcato*—well marked

Brio—vivacity, life, sparkle

Cantabile—in a singing style

Col—with the, e.g. *col arco*—with the bow

Con—with, e.g. *con brio*—with vivacity

Da, dal—from, from the, e.g. *da capo*—from the beginning

Desto—sprightly

Divisi—divided. Used in orchestral music when, for example, the 1st violins are to be divided into two sections playing different parts

Dolce—gently, sweetly

Dolcissimo—very sweetly

E, ed—and

Energico—energetically

Espressivo—expressively

Fine—end

Forza—force, e.g. *con forza*—with force

Fuoco—fire, e.g. *con fuoco*—with fire

Giocoso—jocosely, humorously

Giojoso—joyfully

Grandioso—grandly

Grazioso—gracefully.   *Con grazia*—with grace

Legato (*leg.*)—smoothly

Leggiero (*legg.*)—lightly

Ma—but

Maestoso—majestically

Marcato—marked

Martellato—hammered

Meno—less, e.g. *meno allegro*—less fast

Mesto—sad

Molto—much, very, e.g. *molto adagio*—very leisurely

Mosso—moved, e.g. *meno mosso*—less moved

Moto—motion, e.g. *con moto*—with motion

Non—not, e.g. *non allegro*—not fast

Pesante—heavily

Piacevole—pleasingly

Più—more, e.g. *più lento*—more slowly

Pizzicato (*pizz.*)—plucked.   A direction to a violinist,
   'cellist, etc., to pluck the strings with the finger instead
   of playing with the bow

Poco—a little

Pochetto, pochettino, pochino—a very little

Poco a poco—little by little

Quasi—almost, as if, e.g. *quasi lento*—almost slow

Risoluto—resolute

Scherzando, scherzoso—playfully

Semplice—simply

Sempre—always, e.g. *sempre staccato*—always detached

Senza—without, e.g. *senza ritardare*—without getting slower

Simile—the same, similar

Sordino—mute (of a violin, 'cello, etc.)

Sostenuto—sustained

Sotto voce—in an undertone

Sul, sull', sulla—on the, e.g. *sul ponticello*—direction to violinist, 'cellist, etc., to play with the bow near the bridge of the instrument

Tanto—so much, e.g. *non tanto allegro*—not so fast (as the preceding passage)

Tenuto—held, sustained

Tranquillo—tranquil

Troppo—too much, e.g. *lento, ma non troppo*—slow, but not too slow

Tutti—all

Vigoroso—vigorous

Vivacità—vivacity, e.g. *con vivacità*—with vivacity

Vivo—lively

Volti subito (V.S.)—turn' over quickly to the next page (used frequently in orchestral music)

11. Many of the above are used in combination, as is shown in some instances. Further examples:

Allegro animato—fast and animated

Molto moderato—very moderate speed

Dim. più e più—decreasing the tone more and more

Largo e mesto—broadly and sadly

Vivo ma non troppo presto—lively, but not too fast

12. Note also the following in piano music:

M.D.—*Mano Destra*—right hand (R.H.)

M.S.—*Mano Sinistra*—left hand (L.H.)

U.C.—*Una Corda*—one string. This indicates that the left pedal is to be depressed. On a grand piano this moves the keyboard and the action a little to the right so that the hammers strike only two strings instead of three. Formerly the movement was such that only one string was struck; the original term, though now inaccurate, is still used

T.C.—*Tre Corde*—three strings, i.e. release the left pedal

Con pedale—with pedal. The right (sustaining) pedal is to be used at the player's discretion

Sotto—under. When the hands are crossed this is to show which is to be under the other

ORNAMENTS

1. **Ornaments** are decorations, generally of notes of a melody. They are usually indicated by small notes written before the notes they decorate (these being called the 'principal notes'), or by signs over such notes.

2. The correct interpretation of these signs is often a matter of some difficulty, since the writers of the seventeenth and eighteenth centuries, the period during which they were evolved, do not always express their explanations very clearly. Besides this, the style of the piece concerned is apt to affect the rendering. The explanations which follow do not, therefore, pretend to be exhaustive, but are sufficient to give a general idea of correct treatment.

3. **The Appoggiatura or 'Leaning Note'**

This is written as a small note (♪ or ♩) a step above or below the principal note which it decorates and from which it takes its value. It takes:

    (*a*) half the value of a note (dotted or otherwise) divisible by 2;

    (*b*) two-thirds of a long note divisible by 3;

    (*c*) one-third of a short note divisible by 3.

The appoggiatura is usually slurred to its principal note and receives a slight stress.

Ex. 224

* Note the difference between these. In $\frac{6}{8}$ the dotted minim is divisible by 2, in $\frac{3}{4}$ it is divisible by 3.

4. If the appoggiatura is attached to a longer note tied on to a shorter one, it takes the whole value of the longer note, including a dot if there is one.

Ex. 225

If an appoggiatura appears before a chord, it affects one note only. Usually this is the note next below it, but if the appoggiatura is chromatically raised (ex. 226 (*b*)), or if it is slurred up to the note above (ex. 226 (*c*)), it belongs to the note above.

Ex. 226

5. The word **arpeggio** means 'in the manner of a harp', the notes of a chord on the harp being played one after the other, from the bottom upwards. The sign is ⁙. An arpeggio chord begins *on* the beat, not before it, and each note is held. In full, an arpeggio is usually to be written in demisemiquavers, each note being tied through to the end of the full value of the chord.

Ex. 227

Written

Played

When applied to a chord longer than a crotchet in value, write it first as if for a crotchet and then tie through to whatever notes complete the full value, as at (c) above.*

6. An appoggiatura may be attached to the highest or lowest note of a chord in arpeggio, thus:

Ex. 228

Written

Played

Only when attached to the lowest note do the rules already given as to its value apply. Attached to a top note, it loses whatever is necessary to allow for the arpeggio.

7. The Acciaccatura or Crushed Note

This is written before its principal note as a small note with a stroke through its stem ♪. It comes *on* the beat (not before it) and is played as short as possible. In moderate or fast speeds (*andante* or faster) write it as a demisemiquaver; slower than *andante* as a hemidemisemiquaver. The following workings as for a quaver principal note should be memorised:

Ex. 229   Allegro   Lento

Written

Played

For principal notes of greater value, write the working as for a quaver, and then tie through to the remainder of the value, watching for correct grouping.

* See note on page 121.

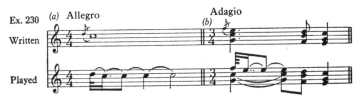

Note (as at (*b*) above) that an acciaccatura applies to only one note of a chord.

8. Acciaccatura and Arpeggio Combined

Write in demisemiquavers (or hemidemisemiquavers if the speed is very slow), with the acciaccatura at the end of the arpeggio.

9. The Pralltriller or Upper Mordent

The sign is ᴧ, placed above the note concerned. The ornament consists of principal note, note above it, principal note again, the first two notes being as fast as possible. (The 'note above' is technically known as an auxiliary note.) The actual note-values depend on the speed of the piece.

(*a*) Slower than *andante* write the first two notes as hemi-demisemiquavers

(*b*) *Andante* and other medium speeds write them as demi-semiquavers

(*c*) *Allegro* or faster, write them as semiquavers.

For longer principal notes, write as above, according to the speed, and tie through to complete the full value.

Ex. 233

10. An accidental placed above the ∿ sign means that the auxiliary note is to be altered accordingly.

Ex. 234

11. **The Mordent** is like the pralltriller upside-down, i.e. principal note, note below ('lower auxiliary'), principal note again. Its sign is ✦. Note-values, etc., exactly as for the pralltriller. An accidental affecting the auxiliary note is placed below the sign.

Ex. 235

It is a common error to refer to ∿ as a mordent. There is no harm in calling it an *upper* mordent, but the true mordent is ✦.

12. **The Turn.** Essentially this consists of four notes—upper auxiliary, principal note, lower auxiliary and principal note again. The sign is ∼.

Distinguish between the turn *over* a note and the turn *after* it. When the sign is written over the principal note, then the turn begins where that note begins. As with the acciaccatura, the pralltriller and the mordent, the essential thing is that it should *sound* quick and so (as with the other ornaments mentioned), the slower the speed of the piece, the shorter the note values of the turn. In any speed below *allegretto* it may be written as a triplet of demisemiquavers followed by a note or notes of longer value, correctly grouped to make up the full value of the principal note.

In *allegro* or faster a triplet of semiquavers suffices.

If over a quaver, or a crotchet followed immediately by another note, it becomes four equal notes:

13. If the turn is preceded by a rest, it begins on the principal note, becoming a quintolet:

14. An accidental above the sign affects the upper auxiliary, below it the lower one.

Ex. 240

Written

Played

15. When the sign is written after the principal note, that note is held as long as possible, the turn coming in quickly at the end. At any speed above *andante* write it as four semiquavers. For *andante* or slower, use demisemiquavers:

Ex. 241   Allegro   Adagio   Lento

Written

Played

This applies also if the principal note is dotted, *provided it does not involve a fraction of a beat.*

Ex. 242

(a) Presto   (b) Andante

Written

Played

(c)

Written

Played

Note the necessary difference in grouping between (b) and (c).

16. If the principal note involves a fraction of a beat, i.e. if it is worth a beat and a half, or three-quarters of a beat, then the simplest method is to make the first three notes of a turn a triplet. The dotted note divides into three equal parts. The first part is the principal note, the second is occupied by the triplet—the first three notes of the turn—and the last part is the principal note again.

Ex. 243 *(a)* *(b)*

At *(a)* the dotted crotchet is worth a beat and a half—three quavers.

At *(b)* the dotted quaver is worth three-quarters of a beat—three semiquavers.

At very slow speeds the triplet can be delayed until the second half of the middle third of the note, its note-values being correspondingly shortened:

Ex. 244

The above renderings also apply with such notations as:

Ex. 245

17. Alternatively, the turn after a fractional dotted note may be rendered thus:

Ex. 246

18. Accidentals affect the turn after a note exactly as they do the turn over a note.

19. **The Inverted Turn** (✦ or ≀) proceeds in the opposite direction to the ordinary turn, i.e. lower auxiliary, principal

note, upper auxiliary, principal note again.   Note-values, accidentals, etc., apply as already explained.

20. **The Shake or Trill.** This consists of a rapid alternation of the principal note and the note above it (*never* with the note below).   The sign is *tr*⌇⌇⌇⌇.   For *allegro* or faster write in semiquavers; for moderate speeds up to *allegretto* write in demisemiquavers; for slow speeds write in hemi-demisemiquavers.

21. A shake begins on its principal note unless:

    (*a*) otherwise indicated by an acciaccatura, which be-comes itself the first note of the shake;

    (*b*) it is preceded by its own principal note.

22. A shake normally ends with a turn unless:

    (*a*) indicated otherwise;

    (*b*) it is short and proceeds to an unaccented note.

At (*a*) the turn is indicated; at (*b*) it is not, but is taken for granted. Note the necessity for the triplet in these, also that it is placed immediately before the lower note of the turn.

At (*c*) the turn is again taken for granted, but no triplet is needed.

At (*d*) the small notes must end the shake, thus avoiding the turn. In this case the triplet comes at the very end of the group.

At (*e*) the shake is short and proceeds to an unaccented note. The quintolet is needed to avoid leaping from the auxiliary note. *The last note of a shake is always the principal note.*

23. Small notes at the end of a shake, as in the preceding examples, are incorporated into the shake, taking the same note-values as the rest of it. But sometimes the last two notes of a final turn appear as full-sized notes, and must retain their printed value. Compare (*b*) with (*a*) below.

24. A shake over a short note proceeding to an accented note generally resembles a turn beginning on its principal note. Over a very short note, unless the speed is very slow, it may have to be reduced to a mere triplet—see ex. 251 (*b*).

25. A shake over two notes affects the upper one only— ex. 252 (*a*). If a double shake is required, two *tr*⌇⌇⌇ signs are needed—ex. 252 (*b*).

Ex. 252

26. Small notes preceding a shake are taken into it:

Ex. 253

27. A shake over a dotted note which involves a fraction of a beat ends 'on the dot', no turn being needed:

Ex. 254

If no fraction of a beat is involved, the treatment is the same as for undotted notes.

Ex. 255

28. An accidental placed above the principal note affects the auxiliary.

Ex. 256

Note the natural to the final A. This note is not affected by the flat in the shake.

29. Older and less common signs for shakes, and one or two other ornaments are dealt with in the Appendix.

EXERCISES ON CHAPTER 17

Write the following passages in full, as they should be performed:

NOTE. *(See page 112.)*

In pianoforte music the arpeggio sign may be used in two different ways. (1) A separate ⸉ for each hand, as at (a), means that the hands begin and finish their arpeggios together. (2) A single ⸉ running across the two staves, as at (b) means that the chord is rolled from the lowest note of the left hand through to the highest of the right hand, the right hand *following* the left.

APPENDICES

1. Sound, in the sense that we normally understand the word, is a sensation of the brain. It is caused by **vibration.** This vibration sets the surrounding air in movement in the form of **sound waves,** which spread out in all directions at once, rather like the skin of a balloon which is being blown up. Some of these waves eventually impinge on the ear-drum. The ear then sends messages to the brain, which translates them into 'sound'.

2. Sound—again in the sense that the word is normally understood —exists only in our brains. As the sound waves get farther and farther away from the vibrating body they become gradually weaker until they finally die of inanition. If there is nobody within earshot, that is, within the range of the sound waves before they have died away, then no sound is actually experienced.

3. The **pitch** of a sound depends on the **'frequency'** of the vibrations, that is, their speed. The greater the speed of vibration, the higher the pitch of the sound. If the speed of vibration is doubled, the pitch rises an octave; if it is halved, the pitch falls an octave.

4. The **intensity** of a sound depends on the **'amplitude'** of the vibrations, that is, their size. The bigger the vibration, the louder the sound. This is easily realised if we watch, say, a 'cellist moving his bow across the string. As the bow is drawn across we shall see that at the point of contact the string appears to swell out. This is the optical effect of the string moving backwards and forwards (i.e. vibrating) at a high speed. If the player exerts greater pressure with the bow we shall hear the sound becoming louder, and the apparent swelling out will increase. As pressure is decreased the sound diminishes, and so does the swelling out.

5. Every musical sound we hear is a compound affair, consisting of the **'fundamental' note**—that is, the note which we hear and can describe as of a certain pitch—and a varying number of other, higher notes which are called **'overtones'** or **'upper partials'**. These, with the fundamental, belong to what is called the **'harmonic series'** of a note. Ex. 257 shows the first few notes of the harmonic series of the fundamental note bass C.

Ex. 257

The pitch of Nos. 7, 11, 13 and 14 is only approximate.

These overtones are, of course, very soft in comparison with the fundamental, but a keen ear may detect a few of them. Depress the right pedal of the piano and strike bass C firmly. A normal ear should be able to hear the third and fifth notes of the series in ex. 257 reasonably clearly. This is a simple proof that they are part of the complex of sounds which go to make up what we call bass C.

6. The **timbre** of a sound depends on the presence or absence, and on the relative strengths, of the overtones produced by the instrument concerned. The nearest approach to a 'pure' sound, i.e. one with no overtones at all, is the tuning fork. The differences between the quality of sounds produced by various kinds of organ pipes is due to the overtones they generate, this being largely conditioned by the material, shape and measurements of the pipes. Not all instruments generate the whole harmonic series; the clarinet, for example, only produces the odd numbers. Trumpets have their higher harmonics strongly developed, hence their brilliant tone.

APPENDIX TO CHAPTER 2

1. The word breve (Latin *brevis*) means short, and it therefore may appear odd that it should be the name of what is now the longest note in use. Since the Middle Ages shorter and shorter notes have gradually come into use and those which were originally long have dropped out. In the days when the breve was really a short note, there were also the Long (Latin *longa*) and the *maxima* or *duplex longa* (double long). The long was worth either two or three breves and the maxima was worth two longs. With the increasing importance of purely instrumental music from the sixteenth century onwards, and the adoption of regular metrical barring, the long and the maxima fell out of use.

2. Semibreve means, obviously, 'half-short' and minim comes from the Latin *minima* meaning 'least' or 'smallest'. The crotchet was at first known as the semiminim.

APPENDIX TO CHAPTER 3

1. The stave originated at some time before the year 1000, as a single red line, representing the note F, drawn above the text of plainsong. Pitch signs called **neumes,** from which our present note-shapes ultimately developed, were written above, below, or across the line. Later a yellow line, representing C, was added above the F line, and still later two black lines were incorporated, one on each side of that for F, thus producing a four-lined stave. Such a stave is still commonly used for the notation of plainsong, the traditional musical chant of the Roman Church.

2. The number of lines used for a stave has varied considerably in the course of the centuries, often at the caprice of the individual composer, and it was not until the seventeenth century that our present five-lined stave became the normal. The Great Stave is purely a theoretical abstraction and, as one writer remarks, 'was never in practical use except by accident'. From our present point of view it is merely a useful way of showing the connection between the treble and bass staves.

3. Clefs began as capital letters. The 𝄞 was actually a capital G which in course of time has come to assume its present shape. Similarly, the 𝄢 was a capital F, and its two dots are all that remain of the two arms of that letter. The C clef, too (see Chap. 14) was originally a capital C.

APPENDIX TO CHAPTER 6

1. Irregular note groups do not necessarily consist of equal notes. For example, one of the notes of a duplet may itself be subdivided as at (*a*) below. A similar procedure may occur with a triplet.

Ex. 258

A more complicated example of irregular subdivision is shown in bar 4 of ex. 259.

2. The regular grouping of beats into twos, threes or fours throughout a piece of music, i.e. into 'bars' of equal length, derives from the regular metrical accentuation of music for dancing. It did

not become the normal in other kinds of music until the seventeenth century. In earlier times vocal music was largely of a character calling for a free rhythm, governed mainly by that of the words. This is clearly seen in plainsong, as well as, for example, in the motets and madrigals of the Renaissance. Such music was unbarred.

3. The so-called 'tyranny of the barline' has persisted until the present day, but in recent years many composers have attempted to break this mechanical regularity of accent by frequent changes of time-signature, so as to achieve greater rhythmic freedom and variety. The English composer Cyril Scott was something of a pioneer in this direction. Ex. 259,[1] from Stravinsky's 'Rite of Spring' shows how a composer may indicate extreme flexibility of rhythm and accent.

Ex. 259

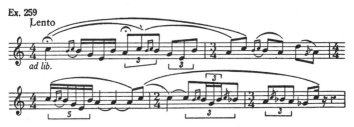

APPENDIX TO CHAPTER 7

1. The French and Italians use a different system of note-names from that employed in this country, and the Germans have also some variation.
2. The following table should be noted:

English	French	Italian	German
C	Ut	Do	C
D	Re	Re	D
E	Mi	Mi	E
F	Fa	Fa	F
G	Sol	Sol	G
A	La	La	A
B	Si	Si	H

It will be seen that the Italian names correspond nearly enough

[1] Reprinted by kind permission of the publishers, Boosey and Hawkes Limited.

to the tonic-solfa syllables for the major scale, the French using
Ut instead of Do, and both using Si instead of Te. The German
system is the same as the English, except that English B is German
H. *German B is English B flat.*

3. The following table gives the foreign names of the various accidentals:

Sign	English	French	Italian	German
♯	Sharp	Dièse	Diesis	Kreuz
♭	Flat	Bémol	Bemolle	Be
×	Double-sharp	Double-dièse	Doppio diesis	Doppelkreuz
♭♭	Double-flat	Double-bémol	Doppio bemolle	Doppel-Be
♮	Natural	Bécarre	Bequadro	Auflösungs-zeichen

4. For the actual names of notes the French and Italians use the
terms given above. The French for B flat is *si bémol*; the Italian
for G sharp is *sol diesis*. But the Germans add *-is* for sharp and
-es for flat. C sharp is *cis*; D flat is *des*. Note that E flat is simply
es, and always remember that in German our note B flat is simply
B. B sharp, of course, is *his*, i.e. 'H sharp'.

APPENDIX TO CHAPTER 9

The following table should be noted:

English	French	Italian	German
Major	Majeur	Maggiore	Dur
Minor	Mineur	Minore	Moll

APPENDIX TO CHAPTER 17

1. Old signs for the **shake** are occasionally met with. The basic
sign is ∿ , indicating a shake beginning on the upper note.

Ex. 260

2. The shake beginning with (*a*) a direct turn, (*b*) an inverted turn:

Note that the direction of the turn follows the direction of its sign.

3. Shake ending with (*a*) a direct turn, (*b*) an inverted turn:

4. Shake preceded by an appoggiatura, which takes its value out of the shake:

5. The **slide** is indicated by the sign for a pralltriller placed in front of the principal note. This principal note is preceded by the two notes below it, scalewise, and these notes take their value from the principal note. Note-values, according to speed, as for the pralltriller.

6. The **after-note** is a very short note which takes its value from the note *preceding* it. It lies between two notes a third apart and is indicated in one of the two ways shown below. Note values as for the acciaccatura.

7. The **extended mordent** has the sign ∿. This is really a short shake: